The Genius of
ANCIENT MAN

Evolution's Nightmare

DON LANDIS
general editor
with *Jackson Hole Bible College*

First printing: October 2012

Master Books®, P.O. Box 726, Green Forest, AR 72638
Master Books® is a division of the New Leaf Publishing Group, Inc.

ISBN: 978-0-89051-677-5
Library of Congress Number: 2012943224

Cover illustration by Ben Iocco "The Battle Over Nephilim"
Design by Diana Bogardus

Unless otherwise noted, Scripture quotations are from the New American Standard Version of the Bible.

Please consider requesting that a copy of this volume be purchased by your local library system.

Printed in China

Please visit our website for other great titles: www.masterbooks.net

For information regarding author interviews, please contact the publicity department at (870) 438-5288

The Pyramid of the Magician
– Uxmal Mexico

PREFACE

Research and studies of ancient man have long been the focus and expertise of the secular world. From evolutionary depictions of cavemen discovering the secrets of fire to New Age shamans proposing mystical alien contact in the distant past, the unbiblical versions of history are many. Meanwhile, the Church has, for the most part, been content to sit back and take no stand on the issue. Accordingly, without any biblical guidance to the contrary, the average churchgoer either accepts evolution as scientific and historical fact or hides sheepishly behind weakly supported Bible stories. But they don't have to be weak; the Church can stand firm on the biblical record if only they will step up and learn the facts.

OOPArts
Out-of-place artifacts

Lake Winnipesaukee mystery stone (left); one of the controversial Ica Stones, Peru (right)

There is real data, and many new archaeological discoveries are presenting evidence for an intelligent ancient man, not one that fits the evolutionary "monkey to caveman" paradigm. All over the world there are similar findings of ancient religions, cities and towers, world travel, advanced astronomy, and civilized government. One can find out-of-place artifacts (OOPArts)[1] and other anomalies[2] that can only be explained by intelligent ancient man. For centuries, these finds have been unknown and unheralded. The Church has since ignored the artifacts, being influenced by an evolutionary mindset that does not allow for advanced ancient technology because it seems impossible to explain.

It is time for Christians to wake up and be instructed. What if mankind is not as ancient as

"science" claims? What if man did not evolve slowly out of slime, completely ignorant and brutish, but rather was created in God's image with a likeness of His intellect? What if Satan is real and actively perverting God's plan? What if man really did gather at Babel, build a tower, form a religion, and instigate a worldwide government? And what if God really did confuse man's languages, forcing the people to scatter across the earth, taking their religion and practices with them? In other words, what if the Bible really is true?

If we read the Genesis account literally, with a consistent hermeneutic[3] (and we believe in the God who wrote it), then we should find evidence demonstrating a history of intelligent ancient man, descended from Adam. In accordance with the scriptural account of Babel, there should be similar building styles and cultural practices all over the earth. These technologies are exactly what is being discovered, and more each day. A jumble of anomalies and magnificent structures continue to confound evolutionary-focused archeology and anthropology today. Yet, as the dots are connected, an incredible picture appears, one that perfectly illustrates history as it is described in the Bible.

Christians, what if your beliefs are actually true? Do you know what it is that your faith actually claims? Do you understand that having a correct interpretation of the Bible influences how you view history and how you should anticipate the future? Did you know that the evidence in the world around you confirms everything you read in the book you call God's Word?

---

1   OOPArts is a term referring to an object that has historical or archaeological significance but exists in an unusual or seemingly impossible context.
2   An anomaly is something that appears to be inconsistent or deviates from the norm; something peculiar or out of place.

---

3   Hermeneutics refers to the rules used in interpreting Scripture. It is important that the rules one employs remain consistent in interpreting the whole of Scripture, not just certain sections.

Jackson Hole Bible College Ancient Man Cruise to Mexico in December 2010.

Well, it's time you knew the answers to those questions and more. This book delves into the fascinating world of ancient civilizations. Discover a time when men could move megalithic stones and build structures beyond imagining, a culture where a new religion was formed and men aspired to be gods, and a world was thrown into confusion by the birth of languages, tribes, and nations.

Over the course of two years, a team of researchers from Jackson Hole Bible College has worked to bring together the different pieces of this convoluted puzzle. Hours of researching, trips to various sites around North and Central America, visits to museums, and meetings with experts have provided the team with an overwhelming amount of evidence for intelligent ancient man. Our goal, to compile information that verifies the accuracy of the text of Scripture, has exceeded our expectations and we have found more than enough evidence supporting our position. Surprisingly, studies by New Age groups have provided much of the data for us. Although our goals and premises greatly differ from these groups, we are able to use the evidence they have discovered to back up our own conclusions. For instance, the New Age groups support the advanced technology and intelligence of supposed

ancient civilizations such as "Atlantis" or Lemuria. We find that these legendary coastal cities and islands fit into a biblical post-Flood era. However, the New Age groups view the demise of these empires as part of the cyclic pattern of world ages whereas we would view the "sinking" of "Atlantis" and the disappearance of other civilizations as evidence of rising ocean levels after the Ice Age.

Through an apologetic method of presuppositions, openly claiming to believe the historical record of the Bible, fully embracing a bias in which we start with a Creator God, this book provides the only plausible explanation of ancient man and his intelligence. The journey has been an exhilarating and enlightening experience for everyone involved. We were continually astounded by the exciting discoveries that continued to provide more evidence confirming our faith. It brings us much joy to complete the final step in our project and present our findings to you.

God has richly blessed us through the Ancient Man Project and has continually provided for us along the way, making each step possible. Now we are thrilled to have this opportunity to invite you to join us and study history as never before.

A Word of Caution

This book seeks to provide evidence that supports the truth of God's Word and confirmation to your Christian faith. However, because of the nature of the subject and the connections that can be made to the occult, we want to warn you to study the information carefully, as the Bereans (Acts 17:11) were instructed, taking everything back to the Bible. For just as Paul says in 2 Corinthians 10:5, we want to encourage you to destroy "speculations and every lofty thing raised up against the knowledge of God" and be careful to take "every thought captive to the obedience of Christ." Some of the data presented includes ancient legends, religions, and cultural practices that we are not promoting, only using them to display further evidence that supports our presuppositions. We would like to caution you as you search deeper into such things, for though they can be used to confirm biblical accounts, such things are not necessarily of God.

As we begin this investigation of ancient man, it is important to always keep in mind the axiom[4] that Satan cannot create, he can only pervert. He must use God's designs and distort them to fit his own plan. We cannot ignore his influence in history and present times. Moreover, we must remember that above all things, Satan longs to be like God (Isaiah 14:14) and hates everything that God does. Satan is actively involved in assuring that God's plan isn't discovered.

Satan distorts everything that God does, inventing an alternate storyline for people to discover, enticing them with lies that seem like the truth. His counterfeits are continuously awarded attention and praise from our culture. Therefore, it is imperative for Christians to be constantly on the lookout for Satan's fabrications, because they can be subtly close to the truth. Often when we discover such a counterfeit, it makes it easier to understand and refute the perversion. Throughout this book you will be introduced to some of the ways that Satan has succeeded in deceiving mankind with a counterfeit in the past and how he is still actively attempting to do so today. (More on Satan's counterfeits in chapter 4.)

We hope you will take great care as you read our material, taking time to allow the truth to seep into your soul and mind. Let yourself question past assumptions. We encourage you to search out the truth for yourself, always relying on Scripture as your starting point and basing your conclusions off of its truth. The Bible is the inerrant Word of God and the complete authority over man: past, present, and future. Therefore, though man does not have all the answers and Satan seeks to confuse us and distort God's plan, he will not succeed. In the end, it is God who has the ultimate victory.

Remember, since the Bible says all men suppress the truth in unrighteousness (Romans 1:18), it is not a question of if there is evidence confirming the existence of God and the authority of His Word. Rather the world knows that God exists — it is only a matter of reminding mankind of the evidence of God's work and the truth of His Word.

JHBC students at Colorado National Monument, examining evidence for the global Flood.

4   At Jackson Hole Bible College, we use the term "axiom" to refer to biblical truths that should be well understood and widely accepted facts in the Christian arena. Please see Chapter 12, page 98 ff for more information and a list of other important axioms.

"Then God said, 'Let Us make man in Our image, according to Our likeness. . . . Then the Lord God formed man of dust from the ground, and breathed into his nostrils the breath of life; and man became a living being"

—Genesis 1:26, 2:7

INTRODUCTION

Like most questions about history, these do not have easy, straightforward answers. In fact, depending on whom you ask, you could get multiple answers from people all equally passionate about their position. You may be tempted to write this book off as "just another theory" and not worth your time, but let us convince you otherwise. This book is different and attempts to explore the topic of ancient man in a whole new light — giving answers based on the Bible.

Who were the people of ancient history? *What* were they like? *What* did they do and *how* did they do it? When exactly did they live?

God's Word is the ultimate starting point for all knowledge and therefore the first place we should be looking for answers to any of our questions (Proverbs 1:7). From the very beginning of Genesis to the last pages of Revelation, the Bible is authoritative in all that it records. The history of mankind and the universe he inhabits is clearly described in the verses of Scripture.

So when it comes to ancient man, we start at the beginning: "Then God said, 'Let Us make man in Our image, according to Our likeness. . . . Then the Lord God formed man of dust from the ground, and breathed into his nostrils the breath of life; and man became a living being" (Genesis 1:26, 2:7). Adam: the very first human being, fully formed and intelligent, designed to perfection, created with a purpose, destined for a future. With this starting point, in contrast to the evolutionary view of man evolving slowly from slime, these facts are interpreted much differently than secular historical science would lead you to believe.

Following the time line of the Bible, a fascinating world appears out of the past. In this world, men lived for hundreds of years (Genesis 5), and a catastrophic worldwide Flood actually happened, cleansing the planet of corruption (Genesis 6–8). Ancient architects built a tower in rebellion to the one, true God, and languages were introduced into the world for the first time, initiating the scattering of the nations (Genesis 11). In the biblical version of history, ancient men were intelligent, building cities, discovering sciences, and exploring the world. With biblical presuppositions in place, the evidence in the physical world around us makes sense and clearly supports this history. The monuments and artifacts that have been discovered today cannot be properly explained by any non-biblical ideas. Ancient architecture around the world testifies to creativity, intelligence, and worldwide communication. The similarities evident in cultures, legends, and building techniques point back to the dispersion of Babel. Such things are a great confirmation of the Bible's truthfulness.

Yet Satan has also made it his purpose to pervert God's truth. His counterfeit storyline has deceived people since those very first days of history and he will not give up until the end of time. He is the "father of lies" (John 8:44), and he is good at it. He has not left history free of his deceptive touch and so we must always be on guard, discerning the counterfeit and standing firm on the truth of God's Word.

The topic of ancient man does not have to be complicated or frightening. In contrast, the truth about ancient man can be both intriguing and encouraging. With the right starting point — presuppositions based on the Word of God — ancient history comes alive with truth. At Jackson Hole Bible College we have a passion for God's Word and the truth it presents. We earnestly desire our fellow Christians to have an understanding not only of ancient times and peoples but to have a foundation upon which to build their entire lives. That foundation for their lives should be the Bible and God's authority in all matters. It starts with reading the very words He wrote for us. Please take the step, turn the pages, and enjoy discovering more about God's plan for man, starting at the beginning. . . .

Antique oak carving of the Green Man, the ancient pagan spirit of woods and forests.

"... *the one whose coming is in accord with the activity of Satan, with all power and signs and false wonders,*"

—*2 Thessalonians 2:9*

Perspectives

At a time not as long ago as many people claim (approximately 6,000 years ago), in the beginning, God created. He spoke the sun, moon, and stars into existence. He formed the earth and all that lives and moves upon it. He created the entire universe, and then He made man. Fashioned from the dust of the earth, mankind was created in the image and likeness of God and given the breath of life. That first man rebelled against God, causing the whole universe to be cursed. God Himself placed the curse of death, decay and sin on the whole of creation. Mankind continued to rebel and God judged the earth through a catastrophic worldwide Flood, preserving only eight people. Still men refused to obey, and in response to their collective rebellion at Babel, God confused man's language, forcing the people to leave the security they had with one other as they were scattered over the earth.

A simple story — ancient history in several short sentences — yet it contains the foundational truths that set human history on its present course and will continue to influence the future to its final conclusion. *If man was made in God's image, then he was created intelligent. If intelligent, then there should be evidence of this intelligence. If man gathered at Babel and God confused man's language as a tool to scatter mankind over the earth, then commonalities and a connectedness will be found in all areas of the planet.* These commonalities will be displayed in religion, construction, and purpose. Aspects of Genesis 1–11, including those at Babel, will be found all over the world: towers, solstice alignments, sun worship, stargazing, sacrifice, and human-centered empire building.

This is exactly what is found. All over the earth one finds anomalies testifying to ancient man's intelligence. The evidence of similarities grows almost daily. It has not gone completely unnoticed.

New-Age Beliefs

The New Age community, with its extremes of occult and shamanism, has been working on the data for some time. They have been amassing information and presenting it to promote their premises and conclusions. Theorizing in mysticism and aliens, these premises and conclusions are diametrically opposed to those of the Christian faith.

The New Age and shaman community does not follow the usual evolutionary time scale, which has man evolving many thousands of years ago; rather, they believe evolution occurred much further back, perhaps a million or more years ago. Their premise promotes the idea that there were previous civilizations on the earth, very old and ancient, before ours. In fact, some teach that mankind goes through cycles or ages along with the earth. Each age rises from the ruins of the last, progressing to great heights in discovery and technology only to be catastrophically destroyed, and the cycle continues.

Their purpose is partly driven by the idea that the ancient men of previous periods left behind the truths and histories of their age for future civilizations of mankind to find. Included in these "secrets" is information that could help in dealing with the future and the end of the present age. The cultic New Age gurus begin with the idea of history going through cycles and as such are preparing for the coming end of their own age. If one goes by the ancient Mayan writings, this will occur December 21, 2012, at which time the earth will be destroyed by fire. The present new-age occultists research ancient legends and histories, tracking these ideas and gathering information. They prognosticate that as the end of this age draws nearer, people need to come together, seek out more data, get in touch with the spiritual world, and thus save themselves.

The Nazca lines in southern Peru are believed by some to be landing zones for alien ships.

Make no mistake about it, these New Agers do not deny evolution; they simply push it back millions of years into the past. In cases such as Erich von Däniken,[1] they claim evolution of our species did not happen on this planet at all but on another and humans were "seeded" here long ago. In Von Däniken's *Chariot of the Gods*, he theorized that mankind was placed here by a highly evolved human species from another world. From a secular standpoint, where man suppresses the truth in unrighteousness (Romans 1:18) and erases God from human history, it is easy to see how some might come up with such erroneous conclusions. After studying all the commonalities of ancient man and his incredible intelligence, it is hard to fault such a fantastic theory. It seems at least slightly more plausible than unintelligent human evolution on earth.

These types of theories make sense to a lot of people today and catch a lot of attention from television channels such as Discovery, National Geographic, and History 2. They are able to gain and maintain a following because there is, in fact, data to back up their ideas. Evidence showing the brilliance of ancient man and the commonality of ancient civilizations doesn't fit with the evolutionary model, so many people will latch on to any arguable explanation.

Unfortunately, the Church has not offered an explanation at all. Believers have let it escape their attention that the raw archeological, anthropological, and historical data exists and must be addressed from a biblical standpoint. Just as in all areas of science, both believers and the unbelieving world have access to the same data. Regrettably, this specific data has, for several reasons, been ignored, and in some cases rejected outright by Christians. Just as mainstream evolutionists have ignored the data because it does not fit their uniformitarian paradigm, the Church has avoided it because it looks strange and meaningless to the truth of the gospel message. Moreover, Christians tend to reject the information out of fear because it is often linked to the cultic expressions of past heritages.

---

1   Erich von Däniken is an avid researcher and successful non-fiction writer pursuing the theory that extraterrestrials visited the earth in the ancient past.

SEVEN DAYS OF CREATION FROM A BIBLICAL WORLD VIEW	DAY 1	DAY 2	DAY 3	
	Gen. 1:1-5	Gen. 1:6-7	Gen. 1: 9-13	
	Earth, Space, Time & Light	Atmosphere and separation of waters	Dry Land & Plants	

However, the sad fact that this data has been studied almost solely in the realm of the occult and New Age movement should not keep Christians from discovering the truth. The secular world has their theories according to their paradigms and presuppositions, but their explanations are not the only ones. Christians do not need to fear the accumulation of data that seems to support secular, mystical theories because the Bible provides the truth. The Christian paradigm is different. The biblical starting point is different. Thus there are alternate conclusions in contrast to the mystical ideas. Christians cannot run from this topic because the raw data is real and cannot be ignored; however, it is important that the evidence is studied from the right perspective in order to discover truth.

A Biblical Perspective

Now put on a different pair of glasses — biblical glasses: the earth is young; history is young. Yet man is indeed moving to an end of this age, a point in time that will not bring on another cycle but rather the end of the entire world. The biblical paradigm rests on the truth of the short narrative related at the beginning of this section. God is real and exists in eternity. He created a beginning of the universe, formed mankind, judged man, and offers a way of salvation. This same God promises a final conclusion of judgment by fire in which this present earth, sun, and universe are destroyed and replaced (2 Peter 3:10–13). Then begins a state that will continue forevermore — no cycles, no ages: eternity. While the history of mankind can be described in short cycles of repeating rebellion against God, judgment, repentance, and restoration, there is only one age of this earth. God has written the story of mankind, both past and future, tracking the "cycles" of man's mistakes and accomplishments. Satan, also a real and active participant influencing mankind, has perverted this idea of cycles and has offered the world an explanation involving millions of years, aliens, and mystical forces. Even though there seem to be hundreds of theories regarding human origins, there are really only two options: God's truth or Satan's lie. Everyone believes one whether they admit to it or not. It is only at the end, when this world is finally judged and utterly destroyed, that everyone will know the truth.

Temple of the Inscriptions, Mexico; design may relate to the departure of the soul at death.

Day 4	Day 5	Day 6	Day 7	
Gen. 1:14-19	Gen. 1:24-25	Gen. 1:26-31	Gen. 2:1-3 Col. 1:17	
Sun, Moon, & Stars	Sea & Flying Creatures	Land Animals & Man	God 'rests' His work of creation Now He upholds His Creation.	

"... be like God,
knowing good and evil."

—Genesis 3:5

PRESUPPOSITIONAL APOLOGETICS/STARTING POINTS

At Jackson Hole Bible College, just as at Answers in Genesis, the method of presuppositional apologetics is employed in evangelism and defense of the Bible. This method assumes a starting point for all beliefs. Every person has a bias, whether they realize it or not; an assumption that influences everything they believe to be true. The ultimate starting point, the bias present in this book, is that God, the Creator of the universe, is real and His Word, the Bible, is entirely true and accurate.

By starting with God, one discovers with great satisfaction that the physical world confirms the truth of His Word. Daily life displays countless verifications of the Bible such as:

Adam and Eve were cast out of the garden of Eden after rebelling against God.

Gen. 3:15–19; James 1:14–15	We find that man's sin and its consequence, as taught in the Scriptures, answers the question of pain, suffering, and evil in the world
Gen. 3; Rom. 8:21–22	Everywhere we look, the death, disease, and chaos inherent to our world testifies to God's Curse on the planet and the introduction of entropy
Gen. 6–8; 2 Pet.	The Flood of Noah's day is confirmed by the fossil record and geologic features of the earth
Eccles.3:11; Rom. 1:25	We find that the universal need for religion confirms that God has set "eternity" in man's heart
Gen. 3–6; Rom. 7:18	Just as the Bible indicates, man, left alone and starting with himself, self-destructs along with his culture and empires
Gen. 6:9; Ruth 1:16–17; Acts 9:18–22; 2 Cor. 5:17	We see in the lives of believers down through the centuries the effects of the regeneration brought by the power and Spirit of God, as men trust in Christ and His work on the Cross

And so it becomes clear that with the right starting point, all the pieces fall into place. Ultimately, the existence of God and the truth of the Bible, interpreted *literally, historically, grammatically, and contextually,* provide the key to explaining the past, how to function in the present, and how to prepare for the future. From this ultimate presupposition come other presuppositions, some of which deal directly with the study of ancient man.

This book is founded on and seeks to confirm three specific presuppositions that support the accuracy and authority of the Scriptures as they relate to ancient man and his practices:

1. **Authorship and authority of the Bible**

2. **Man created intelligently in God's image**

3. **Babel as the origin of similarities, counterfeits**

These three presuppositions provide the outline for this book as each one is expounded upon and supported. Each is a distinct point, yet the three are interlocked and inseparable, overlapping each other, and each is essential for the study of ancient man. The following pages describe the presuppositions separately in hopes to provide a clear understanding of their importance and to emphasize their influence on history.

1. Authorship & authority of the Bible

Since God revealed the text of the Scriptures, then it does not matter when He delivered the text to the men who scribed it. The Bible is the authority, no matter when it was written or who penned it, because God is and has the ultimate priority in sequence and time.

This first presupposition is founded on the ultimate starting point of the eternal, Creator God.

The belief in creation sets forth a sequence in which God exists, dwelling in eternity past. He created all things, including time. This earthly time is limited and prescribed by His ultimate plan, starting with creation and ending with judgment, a new heavens and new earth. After this, eternity continues without time. This is a very important concept, so please read carefully and take time to reread and meditate on this idea.

Again, note carefully the sequence that unfolds based on the biblical presupposition:

God Exists	He Creates	Adam & Eve	They Rebel	God Judges	Babel	Dispersed	One World
—dwelling in eternity past (Isa. 43:13) is the beginning and end (Rev. 21:6)	He creates the entire universe in six literal, twenty-four hour days (Gen. 1-2:3)	He forms Adam and Eve, intelligent & perfect, on the sixth day (Gen. 1:26-30)	They rebel (entropy is introduced into creation) & all succeeding generations pass their now sinful nature on to their children (Gen. 3)	God judges the whole world with a flood, preserving only eight chosen people: Noah & his family (Gen. 6-8)	After several generations, mankind collectively rebels at Babel; begins a one-world religion & government in opposition to God (Gen. 11:3-4)	As judgment, God confuses their languages, scattering them over the face of the earth. (Gen. 11:5-9); mankind takes their form of rebellion with them	One-world government & religion spreads globally, will rise again in the last days to face final judgment from God. (Rev. 16:19, 18:2, 10)

From the beginning, the stories of the original man and woman, their sin, the Flood of Noah's day, and the gathering at Babel were all pieces of history passed down from generation to generation. As each father related the events to his sons and daughters, it would not take long for the story to become distorted, exaggerated, and perverted. The stories spread over the entire globe with the dispersion of the peoples, surviving through the changing civilizations, taking on different cultural twists, becoming the lore of the ancients. Thus, today there are hundreds of legends describing a worldwide flood as well as many creation legends (see chapter 9). From the ancient Mayan civilizations to the aborigines in Australia, cultures all over the earth have similar stories about history. Why? Because they all came from a common source, the original itself! The distortions in legends do not deny the biblical account but rather confirm it with their similarities.

Unfortunately, the secular world does not see the biblical account as the original. Without a presupposition starting with the Creator God, there is no reason to choose one legend over another. Historians throughout the years readily latch on to any one particular story and claim it as the truth. For example Hammurabi,[1] in very early times, set forth one of the

---

1 Hammurabi was the first ruler of Babylonia and was very successful in restoring order and justice to the land of ancient Mesopotamia. The "Code of Hammurabi" was written about 1786 B.C., and some speculate that Moses only revised this code to come up with the Levitical laws.

first organized systems of law. His "code" contains many of the biblical elements of justice that God sets forth in the Mosaic Law, but it also lists many biased, unfair, and even mystical distortions. Yet the secular world sees these first laws of Hammurabi as having more significance than the accounts of the Bible. Why is this? Because Hammurabi wrote his code before Moses penned God's account of the creation, Flood, and the laws by which to govern Israel. With all historical accounts there is this problem — the older a text, the more authority, truth, and viability it has. The older accounts are more enamoring and enticing to the mind. In contrast, the writings of Moses are seen as a sophisticated version of older legends, a revised copy of older accounts.

Yet starting with the paradigm that God was there first, all of these ancient accounts are discredited. Records and documents such as Hammurabi's code unquestionably come from legends and practices passed down through the generations, but the biblical account comes from the source. Moses may have been the hand that wrote Genesis, but a God who created the universe had no trouble conveying that information, without error, to the

Code of Hammurabi/10 Commandments

patriarch. God, as the original author, is the ultimate authority — more reliable than ancients like Hammurabi. As such, Moses' work can be considered the original, free from the errors and distortions that arise from centuries of tradition and story telling.

It is important to understand the priority of God's Word for several reasons. First, if a Christian does not consciously remember and believe the truth of the Bible when he watches a television presentation of ancient civilizations, or reads a magazine article about ancient religions, then he unconsciously begins to assume that these reports have authority. He may inadvertently place this history and research over the biblical account and thus he undermines the authority of Scripture without

knowing it. Over time, this has a devastating effect on his trust in the reliability of Scripture. A struggle takes place in his mind as he tries to adjust what the Bible teaches to what secular history claims.

Another important benefit to a proper understanding of the priority of God in sequence and time is the discovery that the historical data and ancient legends actually verify the truth of Scripture. The distortions that may lead people astray from the truth, when seen as the perversions they are, can provide confidence to Christians because there are clear connections to the real story. God's Word can be trusted as the original, undistorted, and perfectly correct version of history.

Thirdly, there is value for the future as well. If God has written this masterwork of history with a planned beginning and purposeful plot, then it has a resolute conclusion. God's conclusion will be the outworking and fulfillment of His purpose in contrast to the counterfeited purpose of Satan and mankind. Thus, by understanding the past, the core concepts and lies of Babel, one can better understand what to expect at the end of time. This final chapter cannot be ignored, for Jesus revealed the conclusion in Revelation 17. When He returns, the religion and world government of Babel will have risen once more. There will be a world system called Babylon (the fulfillment and completion of the purposes of ancient Babel), known as the mother of abominations and all false religion (Revelation 17:5). The rebellion that began in the early days of Babel will reach its climax in the last days, days like those in the time of Noah (Matthew 24:37–39). And just as in those ancient days, the last days will come to a catastrophic end as God judges the earth for the final time.

This presupposition will be further supported in chapter 4, which gives examples of and insight into Satan's counterfeit of God's plan.

2. MAN CREATED INTELLIGENTLY IN GOD'S IMAGE

Since the Bible is true, God created Adam and Eve in His likeness; therefore they were very intelligent, lived many years, and had great abilities in science, architecture, music, chemistry, spiritual insight, etc. They would pass this intelligence on to their children, creating many generations of very intelligent people.

If this presupposition is true, then evidence that shows the intelligence of ancient man will be discovered all over the earth. It should be impossible to deny the data that will point to ancient civilizations with magnificent capabilities and advanced cultures. If this presupposition is true, then secular ancient history needs to be rewritten.

"Then God said, 'Let Us make man in Our image, according to Our likeness . . .' " (Genesis 1:26). This paradigm stands in stark contrast to the evolutionary premise of early man. The naturalistic model[2] depicts the first humanoid beings as brutish creatures evolving out of slime, looking more like apes than humans. Their behavior would be only slightly advanced above the rest of the animal world from which they were evolving. These advancements could include a slowly developing system of communication, living in caves struggling to discover the secrets of fire, and laboring to move and build things before finally inventing the wheel. Thus, the further back into history, the more the evidence should support unsophisticated ancient civilizations with little to no culture, refinement, architecture, or advanced skills. By going to the Word of God, Christians are able to refute this claim of primitive man with truth that coincides with the physical evidence. The Bible makes a number of claims signifying the intelligence of early man:

▷ He was made in God's image: "Then God said, 'Let Us make man in Our image, according to Our likeness; and let them rule over the fish of the sea and over the birds of the sky and over the cattle and over all the earth . . .' " (Genesis 1:26). Man was the only part of creation that was made in the image of God and therefore

he has qualities that no other created thing can boast. Man carries the "likeness" of God which accords him intelligence, emotions, communication, etc. Further, God states man was to rule over the animals and the earth, therefore giving him a powerful role in creation, requiring a level of intelligence that nothing else was capable of.

▷ He was able to name all the animals: Intelligence is illustrated in Adam's first assignment: naming the animals. "And the man gave names to all the cattle, and to the birds of the sky, and to every beast of the field" (Genesis 2:20). Adam was evidently formed with a creative and efficient mind in order to complete such a task.

▷ He was able to communicate with God: Both Adam and Eve display their intelligence in their ability to hold a conversation with God. Genesis 3:8 says, "They heard the sound of the Lord God walking in the garden . . ." indicating that this was a regular occurrence. When God converses with Adam and Eve, they prove to be completely fluent in speech (Genesis 3:9–12). Evidently God did not create man with the need to learn such things slowly as a child would today.

▷ He demonstrates conscience and knowledge of right and wrong: God gave Adam and Eve a choice right at the beginning: "From any tree of the garden you may eat freely; but from the tree of the knowledge of good and evil you shall not eat, for in the day that you eat from it you will surely die" (Genesis 2:16–17). They were given the opportunity to obey or rebel. Eve also demonstrates that she had the ability to reason and when she "saw that the tree was good for food, and that it was a delight to the eyes, and that the tree was desirable to make one wise, she took from its fruit and ate; and she gave also her husband with her, and he ate" (Genesis 3:6). Immediately, however, they become aware that they have made a mistake and they cover themselves and hide from God (Genesis 3:10). This indicates that they had a conscience and a sense of morality that places them above that of plants or animals.

---

2   Naturalism is an evolutionary theory stating that everything came about by natural processes not allowing for any supernatural influence.

Early on we find occupational abilities: farming, animal husbandry, music, metallurgy, etc.: It was not only the original two humans who were created intelligent. The first children of Adam and Eve, Cain and Abel, show skill and occupational abilities: "Abel was a keeper of flocks [and] Cain was a tiller of the ground" (Genesis 4:2). These early people were quick to make a living for themselves. They had intelligence that helped them in the physical world. Moreover, there were early musicians such as Jubal, "the father of all those who play the lyre and pipe" (Genesis 4:21), proving they had an appreciation for art and beauty. Some were skilled in metallurgy such as Tubal-cain (Genesis 4:22), while some, like Cain, had the incredible skill to design and build cities (Genesis 4:17). These early, ancient men were not dense, dull-witted creatures, but perfectly designed, intellectual beings.

Moreover, due to their long lives (as recorded in Genesis 5), they would have been able to share their discoveries down throughout the ages and work together for long periods of time. If indeed Adam was the most intelligent man to live, then the succeeding generations who lived during his 930 years would have been able to benefit from his teaching and wisdom.

In later chapters of this book, some of the evidences that proclaim the intelligence of ancient man are presented, evidences found all over the earth. The apparent advanced construction, science, religion, and technology baffles modern man today. Viewed from an evolutionary starting point, the evidence does not fit. In contrast, the extraordinary artifacts confirm the presuppositions of the biblical model.

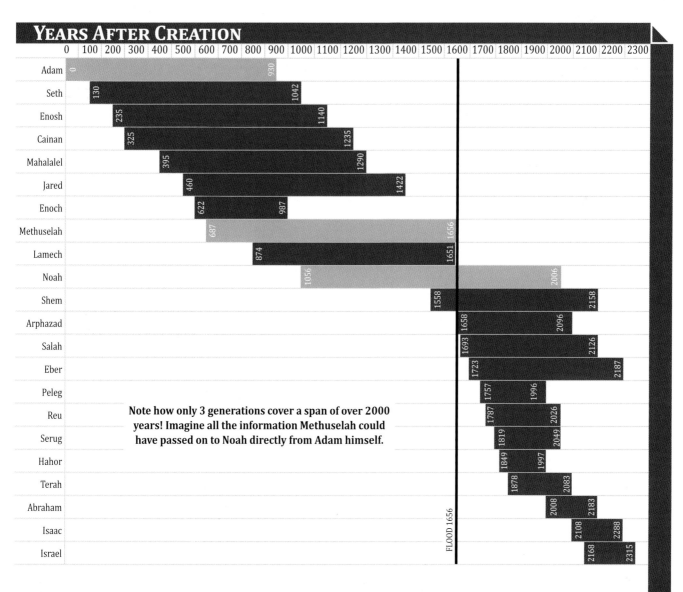

YEARS AFTER CREATION

Note how only 3 generations cover a span of over 2000 years! Imagine all the information Methuselah could have passed on to Noah directly from Adam himself.

FLOOD 1656

3. Babel as the origin of similarities, counterfeits

Since the Bible is true, the rebellion and judgment at Babel did indeed occur and is the source of languages, the reason for the dispersion of ancient man, and explanation for all the similarities in the architecture, religion, and culture around the world.

Just as the second presupposition stands in stark contrast to the natural flow of an evolving world, this presupposition contradicts the idea that each world culture evolved slowly and primarily without influence from other civilizations. It also rests heavily on the truth of early man's intelligence; so much of this specific study of Babel verifies the second presupposition as well. Ancient cultures all over the world show links of intelligence in areas of architecture, religion, mathematical abilities, and astronomical understandings.

Writers and researchers in the secular field marvel at the commonality and similarities of ancient civilizations worldwide. Confirming the biblical account, our research has shown commonalities in everything from construction and calendars to communication and travel. There is even evidence of navigational abilities that were lost for centuries until more recent times. An in-depth study of Genesis and the account of Babel provide a perfect basis for how these commonalities occurred.

Beginning with Eden

It is important to note that the rebellion at Babel did not begin with the building of the tower. It was really set in motion in Genesis 3 with the serpent's first attack on God's Word. Satan deceived man, cast doubt on God's truth, and tempted man with independence; that disobedient bite of fruit was man's first attempt to "be like God, knowing good and evil" (Genesis 3:5). Babel was simply the next step in Satan's plan to undermine God's authority and to become like Him.

One can hardly imagine what it would have been like for Noah's family to step off the ark into a world completely changed and void of all other

human beings. It would be natural for this small group of people to travel together and, for the first number of years, remain a close-knit group. As children were born and grew up and bore more children, slowly expanding the world's population, it would be normal for the families to stay in touch, beginning to farm and settle in close proximity to one another. It would be difficult to imagine families breaking away to wander off great distances, despite God's command to fill the earth (Genesis 9:1). The Bible says this was the case and people generally settled in the land of Shinar. It is on this plain that a call is put forth, a call to gather together and build a city, a call to rebellion.

Seen as a simple Bible story, and generally not given much emphasis or study, the historical significance of Babel usually goes unremarked. Yet it is here in this short narrative that the study of ancient man really begins.

It is possible according to Genesis 10:10 that Nimrod was the founder of Babel. In Genesis 11: "Come, let us build for ourselves a **city**, and a **tower** whose top *will reach* into heaven, and let us make for ourselves a **name**, otherwise we will be scattered abroad over the face of the whole earth" (Genesis 11:4, emphasis added). The call indicates three goals: a city, a tower, and a name.

The first goal was the building of the city itself. The text also suggests that the motivation behind this project had a purpose beyond the three stated goals. Building the city was, in fact, a direct act of rebellion against God. God had instructed Noah to fill the earth, but builders of the tower determined to come together and unify lest they be scattered. This outright disobedience of God's command may seem surprising — after all, these new generations would have grown up hearing stories of the judgment which destroyed all of mankind when he previously rebelled. Yet as the years went by, believing the fantastic accounts of a worldwide Flood would require an increasing amount of faith. No doubt, Noah cautioned the people to stay close to God in their hearts and obey

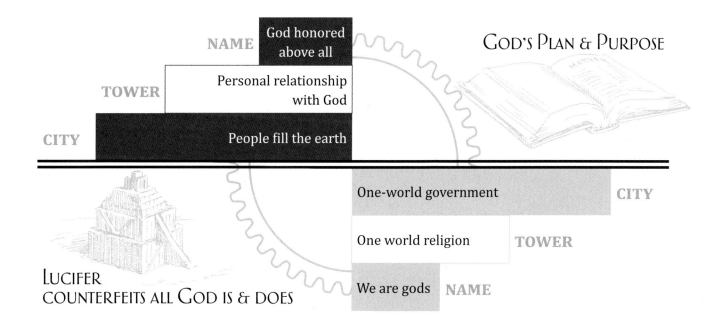

NAME — God honored above all

TOWER — Personal relationship with God

CITY — People fill the earth

LUCIFER COUNTERFEITS ALL GOD IS & DOES

One-world government — CITY

One world religion — TOWER

We are gods — NAME

Him with their actions but, as history has proven again and again, man prefers to make his own way, suppressing the truth in unrighteousness.

And so mankind rejected God and put his faith in the strength of unity. The call to build the city was a direct affront to the command and will of God. In it, man created his own place of safety and security without God. They could benefit from fellowship and pooled resources, be entertained by festivals, and plan for the future together. Man is a social creature, created for fellowship first with God and then with other men. Hermitism is not the norm. As history and culture worldwide demonstrate, there is a desire and a need that lures people to unity and the hope it offers. This desire for unity is not wrong, but the problem arises when man tries to be united while rejecting God. God has a plan in which men work together as part of the body of Christ (1 Corinthians 12:12–26). It is only when men follow God's original instructions that true unity can be achieved.

Remember, Satan cannot create but only pervert. It is certain that he was actively involved in the building of the city, and therefore his influence cannot be forgotten. Yet since only God can create, where did this idea of a city come from? One can trace throughout the Bible that the cities started with God. He has an ultimate plan for the city of

God (Psalm 46:4; Revelation 21:2) and a kingdom built on righteousness (Psalm 89:14). So knowing the importance of cities to God's plan, Satan, in his desire to be like God, perverts the idea and turns city building into a rebellion against God. With the building of that first city, the construction of Babel, the counterfeit began in earnest. Satan's forged story line continues to this day and will become exceedingly more evident as the last days draw near.

At Babel, Satan began the effort of world domination. From the concept of the unifying city comes the idea of one-world government. *This goal has been the underlying premise of countless world powers throughout history, but it began at Babel. Through this concept Satan implemented his next step in his attempt to overthrow the authority of God.*

The second goal at Babel was to build a tower. To understand this significance one must understand the purpose of the tower. The text says it was to be built "to heaven," signifying that it was religious in nature and purpose. It was to be the worship center, the crowning glory of the city. These people were, in fact, beginning something new: a collective, organized, one-world religious system. Of course, since Satan cannot create but can only pervert, the new religious system was only a counterfeit of God's original truth, which had been previously revealed to mankind. Indeed,

Babel

These two interwoven ideas would continue down through history, evident even in present times. Jesus says in Revelation 17 that this ancient religion will resurface in a future religious system that will be carried along by the future political system. As the ancient world order of Babel, to be called Babylon, rises in the last days, the ultimate goal of universal worship will finally be fulfilled under the rule of the Antichrist.

The third goal, making a name, often goes overlooked and unstudied. Builders of the tower knew they needed a core system, something that would be the glue to hold everyone together and motivate their efforts. The "name" would be a world philosophical system of belief in man and in his own ability to succeed. By coming together, mankind bolstered his faith in mere humanity, lifting himself up by his own efforts and uniting in order to build a hope for the future. Perhaps humanism best articulates this mindset, but these ideas can be discerned in many world philosophies. Founded in mankind's abilities, his wisdom, his inventions, his understanding, his discovery, and his analysis, man proposes to find purpose, value, and meaning in life. By offering the people this philosophy, builders of the tower offered freedom from all restraint and secured their support.

a study of the "Mystery of Babylon" will reveal a religion based around a false trinity, female and male cultic worship, sun worship, and numerous other fabrications that are distortions of the truth.

The tower was built to get information and progress the new religion. It was not built as some simplistic, evolving invention of worship. It was a sophisticated attempt, led by Satan himself, to unlock the heavens. The tower was to transport man into a higher realm, to discover and gain a collective understanding of how men could find their way to god-ness. It likely relied heavily on stargazing and astrology, a distortion of God's original purpose for stars found in Genesis 1:14. (See chapter 4 for more information on stars and the horoscope.) Upon further study, it appears the tower was built as a counterfeit mountain (also found in more detail in chapter 4), so even these first ziggurats and pyramids were a distortion of God's original design.

The tower was a call to begin a new system of religion, a system that erased the need for God. Builders of the tower added this goal of one-world religion to their goal for one-world government.

With this threefold purpose encouraging them, mankind united and began to build. They worked, believing they could be rid of God Himself and His will and power over their lives. Never again would they have to fear the wrath or judgment of a God who destroyed their forefathers. Cutting themselves free, they pushed forward to determine their own future. Completely misguided and illogically believing they could overpower the Creator God, they pressed on without fear. But such is the result of man's false conclusions when he suppresses the truth.

In response to this direct rebellion, God came down and judged mankind by confusing their language (Genesis 11:7). Ironically, in thinking they were finally establishing themselves above God, they provoked God into proving to them once again that He is in control. The introduction of languages split the people into small groups, and the resulting confusion forced the groups to separate from each other. The Bible states that the Lord scattered the people across the whole earth. This included not only the rebellious builders but the God-fearers as well. Evidence of the truth they spread is apparent in the distorted myths and legends from around the world.

Yet remember in the hearts of those who had rejected God, the early anti-God movement would not disappear with the introduction of languages and dispersion of the peoples. Rather, the involuntary termination of their building project and forced relocation only proceeded to spread their ideas around the world. Though God's judgment required that they cease the construction of their city, the text does not say the tower building stopped nor the faith in their new creed that man could become god. As the new language groups spread

BABEL
will be called
Babylon in the future.

out, they continued to pursue the three goals with the same fervor and effort as previously. These ideas were embedded in their being. It would not occur overnight, however — as the new civilizations grew in population and strength they would begin to build again. And they did! The various groups built their towers, pyramids, and mounds wherever they went, all linked to their foundation at Babel. As such, today there is evidence of towers built all around the world and a religious system of stargazing and the attempt to get to the heavens deeply entrenched in many cultures. The serpent from the Garden did not give up his plan, but continued to influence the coming generations, always ready to bring what he started at Babel to its ultimate conclusion.

The data proving commonalities of architecture and religion of early man is overwhelming. The extent of worldwide evidence and magnitude of data confirming the text of Scripture must be made known.

Without a doubt, the facts confirm that at the dispersion of Babel, men took their new religion and goals worldwide, resulting in the similarities found today. Many of the commonalities that resulted from the dispersion at Babel are described throughout the coming chapters where they are intricately connected with the evidence of ancient intelligence.

Most of the time, the Church and its theological leadership show little interest in this field. This lack of attention is somewhat understandable, yet a clear comprehension of the past is imperative to understanding what the future holds. Looking forward to the Second Coming of Christ requires studying the past to see what ancient man was doing at Babel. In order to identify the return of Babylon (as Babel will be called in the future), we

The Tower of Babel Stele, 604-562 BC; seems to indicate the Etemenanki ziggurat as the Tower of Babel.

need to study the first world religion formed by Satan and builders of the tower so long ago. So this book has a futuristic purpose, further enforcing the importance of this research. The Church needs to wake up and study its history. In order to prepare for the future, Christians need to know their Bibles, study with a consistent hermeneutic and stand firm on God's Word.

Now that you have an understanding of these three foundational presuppositions, each one will be further supported throughout the book. It is important to always keep all of them in mind while reading because they are so interwoven with each other and throughout the chapters. As you continue to read, prepare to be blown away, yet also comforted, by how much real data and evidence there is which confirms the Word of God.

With the context and understanding of the presuppositional points made in Chapter 2, when you review highlights of ancient and early history, it is easy to see commonalities in architecture, religion, and more. This chapter is a brief visual timeline from Creation to the 1600s that highlight some of the art, ruins, and cultural developments of mankind.

chapter 3

4004 BC
In the Beginning: God starts His plan and purpose of world/human history

▶ *Creation* ▶ *Adam, Eve* ▶ *Lucifer falls-rebels* ▶

▶ *Fall of Man - join Lucifer in Rebellion* ▶ *Cain, Abel*

3874 BC

Seth- beginning of animal husbandry, agriculture

Jubal, Tubal-cain- beginning of music, metallurgy

2948 BC

Noah born

2347 BC

Global Flood   Ice Age begins to build up

2242 BC

Tower of Babel, languages, dispersion

Satan initiates his organized earthly kingdom

2234 BC

Babylonian civilization forms

Pottery jar from the Ubaid period in Mesopotamia in Southern Iraq

Painting of giant deer (Megaloceros giganteus) in the Lascaux caverns

Statue of dancing girl from Mohenjo-daro; early Indus Valley site like Meragh (which showed evidence of bitumen use for waterproofing & drills used in dentistry)

2188 BC

Egyptian civilization forms (Mizraim)

Zodiac "invented"

2089 BC

Grecian civilization forms

c.2070 BC

First Chinese dynasty

Civilizations form in India

24

PRIORITY OF GOD
IN SEQUENCE AND TIME

c.2000 BC

Great Pyramid built

Other megalithic building begins globally

1822 BC

Egyptian letters invented

1810 BC

First Assyrian Empire (Assur)

c.1790-1750 BC

Code of Hammurabi written

1715 BC

Joseph made governor of Egypt

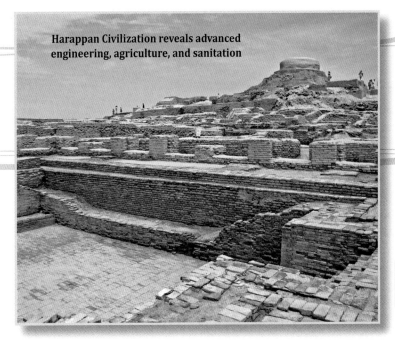

Harappan Civilization reveals advanced engineering, agriculture, and sanitation

c.1650 BC

Ice Age ends, coastal cities disappear in rising ocean levels.

c.1500-500 BC

Book of Job is written

1491 BC

Exodus from Egypt

Moses receives the Law from God (Mt. Sinai)

לא תרצח | יי
לא תנאף | היה
לא תגנב | שא
לא תענה | את
לא תחמד | את

c.1200 BC

Troy is destroyed

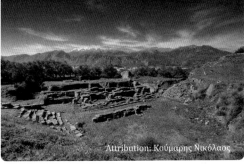

Attribution: Κούμαρης Νικόλαος

A theater in the ancient Greek city-state of Sparta

1096 BC

First king of Israel (Saul)

1048 BC

David becomes king of Israel

c.1000 BC

Sparta built

1000-600 BC
Phoenicians sail the seas, possibly cross the Atlantic

1004 BC
Solomon's Temple built in Jerusalem

931 BC
Israel and Judah split

c800 BC
Homer writes; alludes to Atlantis

748 BC
Rome founded

700 BC
Great Dam of Marib built (Arabia)

The current dam in 1986

721 BC
Israel scattered

586 BC
Temple destroyed, Judah in captivity

A stone with Hebrew writing "To the Trumpeting Place" uncovered during archaeological excavations by Benjamin Mazar, believed to be a part of the Second Temple complex

c520 BC
Jewish Temple rebuilt

400 BC
Nazca civilization (Peru)

367 BC
Aristotle taught by Plato

c300 BC
Glass lenses invented

356 BC
Alexander the Great born

287 BC
Archimedes invents the water screw & lever

248 BC
Iraq batteries constructed/in use

348 BC
Plato dies; wrote about Atlantis

c220-206 BC
Great Wall of China construction

c150 BC
Antikythera Mechanism is in use

70 BC
Water mills used grind grain

19 BC
Herod renovates Jewish Temple

4–5 BC
Jesus Christ is born

2 AD
Rice cultivation starts in Japan

70 AD
Rome sacks Jerusalem

100 AD
Paper invented in China

30 AD
Christ's crucifixion -resurrection

c100 AD
Aztec civilization thrive in Mexico city of Teotihuacan built

122–128 AD
Hadrian's Wall built (Britain)

132 AD
Seismograph is invented (China)

220 AD
Gunpowder made in China

250-900 AD
Mayan civilization - Chichen Itza and other Mayan pyramids built

404 AD
Jerome's Latin Vulgate – translates Bible to Latin

570 AD
Muhammad born, founder of Islam

725 AD
Mechanical clocks used in China

1045 AD
Movable type in China

1070 AD
Great Serpent Mound built

1097 AD
First Crusade

800–1300 AD
Mississippian culture flourishes (Monk's Mound and Woodhenge)

1250–1500 AD
Moai of Easter Island formed

1348 AD
Bubonic Plague kills 2/3 of Europe

1382 AD
Wycliffe translates Bible into English

1400 AD
Machu Picchu in Peru

1440 AD
Gutenburg printing press

1492 AD
Columbus crosses the Atlantic

1513 AD
Piri Reis compiles his map, depicting part of Africa, South America & maybe Antarctica

1517 AD
Martin Luther's Ninety-Five Theses - Protestant Reformation begins

An early printing of Luther's hymn A Mighty Fortress Is Our God

1531 AD
Oronteus Finaeus compiles his map, supposedly depicted Antarctica without ice caps

1600 AD
Early robotic dolls in Japan

a replica of a telescope attributed to Galileo

1609 AD
Galileo uses telescope for astronomy

1620 AD
Pilgrims arrive at Plymouth in America

1631 AD
Taj Mahal constructed (India)

1666 AD
Isaac Newton discovers law of gravity

SOMETIME IN THE FUTURE:

It appears according to Revelation 17:5-6 Jesus uses the name of Babylon to indicate a future fulfillment of what started at Babel.

END OF TIME:

Christ's kingdom comes to earth and history as a compilation of man-made events and governance ends.

chapter 4

"*For our struggle is not against flesh and blood, but against the rulers, against the powers, against the world forces of this darkness, against the spiritual forces of wickedness in the heavenly places. Therefore, take up the full armor of God, so that you will be able to resist in the evil day, and having done everything, to stand firm.*"

—*Ephesians 6:12–13*

Two Kingdoms and the Counterfeit

The history of man is not a catalog of random changes and events. It is a plan, set in motion by the God who created the universe. As He speaks through Isaiah: "I am God and there is no one like Me, declaring the end from the beginning and from ancient times things which have not been done saying, 'My purpose will be established, and I will accomplish all My good pleasure'" (Isaiah 46:9–10). But the plan is not without opposition. Satan has been attacking God's original purposes since the very beginning. Remember, Satan is a part of God's created world; he was given a choice to follow God or not. He rebelled and has since enticed man to follow him. Satan is not infinite or all-powerful, but he wants to be; he desires to be like God. He cannot create, but he actively perverts God's plans and purposes, making them seem like his own. He tries to appear like God, but he is NOT and so those who follow him and his plans self-destruct. God's plan was to create man for fellowship, but Satan deceived man into rebellion and rejection of God.

There are only two religions in this world. One instigated by the true God, infinite, omnipotent Creator of the universe, and leads to eternal life. The other was started by a counterfeit god in opposition to the truth, and ultimately results in death. In Matthew 7, Jesus clearly outlines the two. Through symbols of the narrow and wide gate, the tree and its fruit, and two foundations, Jesus displays the differences between the choices.

The wide gate of Satan's rebellion leads to destruction, while the narrow gate leads to life. The bad tree, Satan's kingdom, can only produce bad fruit, whereas if you eat from the good tree of Christ, you will get only good fruit. Building on God's foundation of rock will allow you to stand firm, while a foundation of sand, based on Satan's weak promises, will fall in terrible destruction. *There are two opposing kingdoms being run here; everything in life is sourced in one of these two kingdoms; everyone must choose which kingdom to be a part of, to follow God or Satan.* There is no in-between; all religions outside of the true faith in the real God have their basis in Satan and his counterfeit religion. There are only two choices: life or death.

Satan has learned to craftily portray his counterfeit kingdom in a way that people often do not recognize. Most of mankind has fallen into his ways and lives in his kingdom. They worship and serve him without even realizing it. The counterfeit plan of Satan has become so ingrained in society that it is heralded as "science" or "philosophy" and taught in schools around the world.

In the biblical worldview, because God created all things, everything starts with God; God has priority. All things originating from God would be good and holy, yet anyone will testify that the world is anything but good and holy! This is due to man's rebellion against God, the introduction of sin, and the curse placed on the world. Furthermore, Satan, in his desire to be like God, works to counterfeit all God is and does, influencing mankind to do the same. Nothing that God loves or uses for His purposes escapes Satan's perversion. Throughout the ages, Satan has attempted to twist, distort, and soil every original concept of God. Yet because these are all distortions, they will contain a seed of the truth; a core concept that is good but has been perverted. That is the nature of a lie; it is not independent but is the distortion of an original truth.

This chapter will describe several examples of how Satan has perverted something from God's plan and used it for his own purposes in his alternate kingdom. There are hundreds of these distortions and, as you learn to be on the lookout, you will begin to see them everywhere in the world around you. Never forget that there is a battle going on and forces from both sides are at work. God does not want His people to fall prey to Satan's lies. We are commanded to put on His armor, resist, and stand firm!

MAN-MADE MOUNTAINS

It is interesting that the original world religion, starting at Babel, centered on the building of a tower. All over the world there are tall religious structures. From the pyramids of Egypt to the pagodas of Japan to temples of Mexico; man seems to have a fascination with building toward the sky. Something must have been encouraging this trend! Graham Hancock reveals that the Edfu texts from ancient Egypt tell of the "builder Gods" whose principle task "was to construct 'sacred mounds' at key locations throughout the land of Egypt."[1] It is evident that ancient people all over were working toward a similar goal, which must have come out of Babel. But where did the builders of Babel first get the idea? As has been discussed previously, Satan was a key player in the rebellion at Babel and likely instigated the tower-building. Since Satan cannot create but only pervert, the origin of these towers must come back to God. Notably, the Tower of Babel was built for religious purposes and therefore gives a hint as to where the idea came from. God had to be the first to instigate worship on high places, namely mountains, and so it is probable that these towers and mounds were simply counterfeit mountains made to worship God or another deity. Though the Bible does not give us the specific instance in which God started using mountains in this way, Satan knew that God had a special purpose for mountains and it was his aim to distort this plan.

Mount Fuji

Chichen Itza

1 Graham Hancock, *Heaven's Mirror* (New York: Crown Publishers, 1998), p. 225.

Gen. 22:2	Abraham was commanded to sacrifice Isaac *on a mountain*
Exod. 3:1-6 Exod. 19:3	God appeared to Moses in the burning bush at *Mount Horeb* and Moses later *climbed a mountain* to meet with God at Sinai
1 Kings 19:11-12	God passes by Elijah on a mountain
1 Kings 14:23, 2 Kings 12:3, 14:4, 15:4, 17:9	God commanded the Old Testament kings to lead the people in tearing down the *high places* where they were worshipping falsely. It was symptomatic of the lack of devotion to God to allow the influences of Babel to remain around Jerusalem.
Ps. 2:6	God installs His King upon Zion, *His holy mountain*
Ps. 3:4	God speaks to the Psalmist from *"His holy mountain"*
1 Kings 18:20-40	God defeats the prophets of Baal on *Mount Carmel*
Ezek. 40:2	God gave Ezekiel a vision from a *very high mountain*
Matt. 14:23 Matt. 5:1 Matt. 17:1-2 Matt. 28:16	Jesus often went up on a *mountain* to pray and be alone or teach. He was transfigured on a mountain and He met the disciples after the resurrection on a *mountain* in Galilee
Dan. 2:34-35, 44-45	Daniel indicates the future Coming and the Kingdom of Christ is like a stone cut without hands that comes and destroys human world government and then *becomes a mountain*
Ps. 48:1 Ps. 68:16 Isa.11:9 Isa. 57:13	The word mountain is often a figurative symbol of the Kingdom of God: "... Great is the Lord, and greatly to be praised, in the *city of our God, His holy mountain*" "Why do you look with envy, O mountains with many peaks, at the *mountain which God has desired for his abode?* Surely the Lord will dwell there forever" "They will not hurt or destroy in all *My holy mountain*, for the earth will be full of the knowledge of the Lord..." "...He who takes refuge in Me will inherit the land and will posses *My holy mountain*"
Heb. 12:22	*Mount Zion* is "the city of the living God, the heavenly Jerusalem"

Interestingly, there were likely no great mountains before the Flood (though Genesis says the waters covered the high mountains, these could not have been as large as today because there is not enough water on earth to cover them.) Psalm 104:8 says, "The mountains rose; the valleys sank down," and many believe that this refers to the draining of the Flood. The immense mountain ranges that are now on earth were formed as a result of God's judgment on mankind. They serve as a reminder to man of sin, the Curse, and even the judgment to come. In the future, the mountains will again be made low (during the tribulation earthquakes occur and cause so much destruction that "the mountains [are] not found" (Revelation 16:20)) save for the mountain of God (Isaiah 2:2, 40:4; Micah 4:1).

It is not only counterfeit mountains that Satan has used for his own religious purposes, but real mountains as well. For example, Emei Shan is a sacred Buddhist mountain (previously sacred in Taoism) in China, and the site of many temples throughout history. In England, Glastonbury Tor is said to be the site of ancient rituals and holds the interests of ley-line enthusiasts with all its mystical associations. Macchu Pichu in Peru, a high mountain ridge, is the mystical site of many ancient temples and palaces. The most holy mountain in

Indonesia, Mount Agung, is home to the largest and holiest temple in Bali, the Mother Temple of Besakih. Japan has many holy mountains, Mount Fuji being the holiest, named after the Buddhist fire goddess Fuchi. Mount Kailash in the Himalayas is a sacred mountain to Hindus, Buddhists, Jains, and followers of Bon. The Native Americans of California regard Mount Shasta as the center of creation, and present-day New Agers believe the mountain to be a source of mystical power. There are hundreds more of these "sacred mountains" that have importance in different religions around the world. And of course there are many biblically significant mountains such as Sinai, Horeb, and Zion.

All through the Old and New Testaments there are examples of God's use of mountains. This was evidently a concept that Satan attacked early on and there are many biblical accounts of Satan perverting mountains. Starting with the tower at Babel, the Bible also records that the pagan nations of Canaan served their gods "on the high mountains and on the hills" (Deuteronomy 12:2), and Israel continually fell into sin by worshiping on the high places (1 Kings 3:2, 14:23). Satan also created conflict between the Samaritans and the Jews through mountains as the Samaritan women reveals: "Our fathers worshiped in this mountain, and you people say that in Jerusalem is the place where men ought to worship" (John 4:20).

Outside the biblical record, it is clear Satan has been actively working to pervert the purpose of mountains as well. All over the world there are more examples of this early counterfeit seen in the hundreds of pyramids and mounds. Yet the idea of mounds, pyramids, or high places did not start with Satan. Always remember that the counterfeiter cannot create, but can only pervert God's ideas. Satan has almost completely distorted the biblical purpose of mountains by incorporating it into his diabolical worship system, creating counterfeit mountains around the globe. Yet even though his counterfeit is so prevalent, God still has priority in time and, therefore, the idea must have started with Him.

STARS, ASTROLOGY, AND THE HOROSCOPE

A market research study discovered that 98 percent of Americans know their star sign and 66 percent read astrological columns regularly.[1] The tantalizing prospect of discovering your future through reading the stars is not a new idea. Later on in this book the examples of ancient man's interest in the stars and advanced astronomy prove that this fascination is an old one. In pride and fear, people of every generation desire to know what the future holds, and for some reason they believe the stars affect and have influence on our lives here on earth. Where did this idea come from and why is it so prevalent in so many cultures all over the world from ancient history to present time? It seems so mystical and eerie that it must be of Satan — but remember, he is unable to create anything on his own, he is only able to pervert what God has created.

The Bible makes it clear that God does have a purpose for the stars. Psalm 147:4 records, "He counts the number of the stars; He gives names to all of them." God even "leads forth their host by number" (Isaiah 40:26) and fixed the "order of the moon and the stars" (Jeremiah 31:35).

God doesn't do anything randomly or without reason, so the names God gave to the stars and their movement in the sky must be significant. Of course, it is impossible for us to know all of the names or understand their significance, but the possibility of discovering their purpose is so enticing that whole religions have been formed around the search. Even the constellations have their roots in God's plan. In three different passages God is given credit for making and controlling Pleiades and Orion (Job 9:9, 38:31; Amos 5:8) and the Bear (Ursa Major) (Job 9:9). Genesis states that God made "lights in the expanse of the heavens to separate the day from the night, and [to] be for signs and for seasons and for days and years" (1:14). The Hebrew word for "signs" means "a mark" or "omen." The stars are notations (marks) in the sky; signs for something! Regardless of God's purposing in creating and naming the stars, Satan has corrupted our understanding of it, getting people to fear the lights of the heavens and look to them for guidance instead of their Creator. (Additional information on the stars is available from Pastor Don Landis).

Regardless of God's purposing in creating and naming the stars, Satan has corrupted our understanding of it, getting people to fear the lights of the heavens and look to them for guidance instead of their Creator. Instead of trusting God with the future, mankind has continually attempted to discover and predict it on his own, often using the stars. The Bible is not silent on this matter. Moses warned the people not to worship the heavenly lights: ". . . beware not to lift up your eyes to heaven and see the sun and the moon and the stars, all the host of heaven, and be drawn away and worship them and serve them, those which the Lord your God has allotted to all the peoples under the whole heaven" (Deuteronomy 4:19). Furthermore, Jeremiah counsels not to be terrified by the signs of the heavens (Jeremiah 10:2). It is clear that man has always struggled with this temptation to find the future in the stars. Satan has truly distorted God's original truth in the night sky, but God still has a purpose for the stars and their constellations that can never be destroyed by Satan's counterfeit.

1   Robert Lomas, "Charlatans, Fortune Tellers, and Soothsayers," accessed November 6, 2011, http://www.turningthesolomonkey.com/?s=why_astrology.

COUNTERFEIT 3

FACING EAST

Around the world, temples and other religious structures are found to be astronomically aligned (which coincides with man's fascination with the stars as mentioned previously), many of them facing east. For example, the Sphinx is aligned gazing due east as well as the temple of Amen-Ra at Karnak and the Gateway of the Sun in Bolivia. The Masonic temples all face east as well as many ancient Greek temples. But why? What is so important about the east that would cause this practice around the planet?

Of course the originator must be God. Indeed, it was God who first placed importance on the east. The garden where God placed Adam and Eve was "toward the east, in Eden" (Genesis 2:8) and it was on the eastern side of the garden that He placed the cherubim.

Throughout the Bible "east" is significant:	
Lev. 16:14	The blood of a sacrificed bull was sprinkled on the east side of the altar (and in front): "Moreover, he [Aaron] shall take some of the blood of the bull and sprinkle it with his finger on the mercy seat on the east side"
Num. 10:5	The tribes of Israel that were camped on the east were the first to march out when moving to a new site: "But when you blow an alarm, the camps that are pitched on the east side shall set out"
Gen. 29:1 1 Kings 4:30	The "sons of the east" were notable and considered very wise: "Solomon's wisdom surpassed the wisdom of all the sons of the east and all the wisdom of Egypt."
Ezek. 43:2, 4, 17 Ezek. 47:1	When the Lord comes to the temple in Ezekiel, He comes from the east and approaches the east gate. The temple steps face east and water flows out from the temple to the east
Matt. 2:1	The magi who visited Jesus were from the east

It is interesting to note that Noah and his family "journeyed east [and] found a plain in the land of Shinar and settled there" (Gen. 11:2). Did God draw upon cultures to use this or did the secularists draw upon God. God is not stealing ideas from the pagans.

God originally placed importance on the east, starting with the Garden of Eden, and Satan has latched onto this idea and influenced many religions to make "facing east" a part of their practices. It becomes something common and connected to pagan religions, and in this way Satan tries to undermine God's purpose for the "east."

COUNTERFEIT 4

HUMAN SACRIFICE

When one thinks of human sacrifice, horrible images come to mind. There are stories of pagan cultic practices where humans are sacrificed to gods or cannibals undergo rituals of eating the flesh of their enemies. Everything from long painful tortures to strange ceremonies resulting in a submissive death, terrify people and are labeled as barbaric and evil. Yet throughout history legends of such practices abound. The Aztec people of Mexico had sacrificed an estimated 250,000 people by the beginning of the 16th century.[1] The Pyramid Texts of ancient Egypt hint that rulers may have made human sacrifices to gain the powers of the gods. In many cultures, human deaths were required to appease a god or used as a way to keep political control. Even the Bible gives accounts of human sacrifice! Both Ahaz and Manasseh, kings of Judah, sacrificed their own children to the god Molech. Whatever the reasons of the past, no one in this generation accepts this manner of killing other human beings and it is considered both disturbing and disgusting.

It may come as a surprise then that this idea of human sacrifice originated with God.

As early as Genesis 3:15, God gives the first prophecy alluding to Jesus Christ's sacrifice. Then in Genesis 22:1–14, Abraham is told to sacrifice his son Isaac to prove that he feared God (yet God stops him from actually killing his son). This story is a foreshadowing of God's own plan to sacrifice His one and only Son on the Cross for all of humanity. Indeed, God had planned this ultimate sacrifice before the creation of the world: ". . . knowing that you were not redeemed with perishable things like silver or gold from your futile way of life inherited from your forefathers, but with precious blood, as of a lamb unblemished and spotless, the blood of Christ. *For He was foreknown before the foundation of the world,* but has appeared in these last times for the sake of you" (1 Peter 1:18–20, emphasis added). Moreover, we were chosen to be saved "in Him *before the foundation of the world"* (Ephesians 1:4, emphasis added), and that is "according to His own purpose and grace which was granted us in Christ *from all eternity"* (2 Timothy 1:9, emphasis added). God's plan of a human sacrifice to save all mankind from their sins was from before time. Moreover, He illustrated this plan through the sacrificial system of Israel. The constant animal sacrifice for atonement for sins was a type of Christ's all-atoning death to come. His amazing sacrifice was one of humility and grace, a beautiful and unmatched action of love. Satan has perverted the idea of human sacrifice and caused the gruesome and terrible deaths of millions of people. But it is only in God's plan that human sacrifice actually has purpose and is truly the cause of worship.

Skeleton of a family in an ancient sacrifice pit in China.

1   Graham Hancock, "Blood and Time at the End of the World," accessed November 8, 2011, http://www.bibliotecapleyades. net/egipto/fingerprintgods/fingerprintgods03.htm.

COUNTERFEIT 5

LIGHT

Yet Satan has taken the concept of light and attempted to use it for his own purposes. The Bible tells us that Satan comes as an angel of light (2 Corinthians 11:14). It is all part of his deception and even "his servants also disguise themselves as servants of righteousness" (2 Corinthians 11:15). Satan knows the connection between light and righteousness and he knows how to take advantage of it. In addition, Satan is called the "star of the morning," wanting to ascend to the heavens "above the stars of God" (Isaiah 14:12–13). Of course, this continues in the idea that Satan counterfeits everything. Satan is not light and is in fact against the Light but he comes masquerading as good, bright, and beautiful. Because God uses light as a symbol of Himself and His holiness, Satan latched onto the idea and uses it to deceive.

Throughout the Bible, God uses light for various purposes.

Job 24:13; Prov. 4:18	Light, in contrast to darkness, symbolizes God's way, the way of righteousness
Ps. 44:3	God says that in His presence there is light.
Ps. 104:2	He covers Himself in light
Ps. 119:105	God's word "is a lamp to [our] feet and a light to [our] path"
Ps. 119:130	"the unfolding of [His] words gives light; it gives understanding to the simple"
Dan. 2:22	Daniel states that light dwells with God
1 John 1:5	John states that "God is light, and in Him there is no darkness at all"
Isa. 9:2	Jesus is prophesied as the coming light
John 1:9	John calls Him the "true Light which, coming into the world, enlightens every man"
John 8:12, 9:5	Jesus Himself declares that He is the "Light of the world"
Isa. 60:19; Rev. 22:5	In the future kingdom of God, His mere presence will be the only light needed

Furthermore, just as Israel was called a "light to the nations" (Isaiah 42:6), Jesus told the disciples that they were the "light of the world" (Matthew 5:14). Also, Christians are told to put on the "armor of light" (Romans 13:12) and to "walk in the Light as He Himself is in the Light" (1 John 1:7). Also, both the "gospel of the glory of Christ" and the "knowledge of the glory of God" are referenced as light (2 Corinthians 4:4, 6). Christians are called "children of Light" (Ephesians 5:8) and "sons of light" (1 Thessalonians 5:5). Clearly, light is closely connected with God, His glory, His word, and His people.

COUNTERFEIT 6

RAINBOWS

In searching for the counterfeit of this, many believers may immediately think of the gay/lesbian rights movement that has claimed the symbol. Or perhaps leprechauns and pots of gold come to mind. These are indeed ways in which Satan is perverting God's symbol of grace, but they are not the only ones. Not all Christians realize that Satan has commandeered this symbol and is using it specifically to symbolize his kingdom as well. The "Rainbow People" who meet on a regular basis in the United States celebrate the rainbow and claim it has rather interesting symbolism. They believe it represents the division of world religion, which came from one pure light and will someday be brought back together under the leadership of one person. They are looking forward to the coming of a "prism" — a man who will unite all religions into one. Of course, most Christians would identify this as the coming antichrist who will attempt this process and have some success in the last days. It is all part of Satan's attempt to overthrow God's people and the Kingdom. Interestingly, it seems to be undeniably connected to the dispersion of the one-world religion at Babel and the goals that began there. This division of world religions the "Rainbow People" talk about was due to the dispersion at Babel! Ironically, in attempting to create their own theories, these people have only confirmed the biblical account and linked themselves to the perversion of Babel. And so again, here is an idea that originated with God but is now used by the enemy in a perverted way.

Rainbow Gathering trader circle. July 5 at the 2005 Rainbow Gathering in Cranberry, WV.

When a Christian sees a rainbow he is mostly likely reminded of God's promise after the Flood of Noah. But it is also common knowledge that rainbows are the result of light passing through droplets of moisture at a certain angle. Pure white light splits into this stunning spectrum when it is refracted through a prism. Though rainbows can be explained scientifically and they occur naturally in the world due to this property of light, God had a special purpose for rainbows in the beginning.

God used the rainbow as a sign of His promise that there would never be a worldwide flood like the one in Genesis 6 thru 8. In fact, it was to be a continual reminder of the covenant that God made with every creature of the earth to never destroy all life with a flood again (Genesis 9:11–17). Of course, this would have been a shallow symbol if Noah had ever seen one before, but since it did not rain before the Flood, the magnificent new phenomena had significant purpose. Ever since, when Christians look up into the sky after a rain and see that sign, they are reminded of God's promise: "I set My bow in the cloud, and it shall be for a sign of a covenant between Me and the earth" (Genesis 9:13).

Furthermore, the Bible uses the rainbow in descriptions of the throne of God. In Ezekiel's vision, he said the radiance around the throne was "as the appearance of the rainbow in the clouds on a rainy day" (Ezekiel 1:28). John also says "there was a rainbow around the throne" (Revelation 4:3) when describing his vision of heaven. God uses this beautiful spectrum of colors around His own throne!

Even from these few examples it becomes clear that all the basic elements of false worship and the evil empire of Satan are counterfeits of the original truth — the plan of God. Little things all throughout the religions and cultures around the world contain Satan's distortions of the truth. Yet because of this, they still contain some truth; God's plan is not completely wiped out but rather confirmed by the links in the counterfeit. Thus, God has priority. He is the first, eternal, always. His purpose and plan and the play He has written has been twisted, distorted, and mutilated, but it can still be traced throughout the ages. It's typical of Satan to spin the truth to the opposite, to make the ancient pagan religions seem to be the original and the Bible appear incorrect. And the world feeds on legends and stories of ancient man. Satan uses these old cultures to claim his own truth and his own beginning, and to mislead mankind away from the truth. But Christians should see these distortions as they are: counterfeit. Christians should have an immune system to Satan's revisions and stand firm against the manipulations of the original truth about God and His work in creation. Remember — Satan distorts God's truth but he can't destroy it. The truth is there even if depraved mankind continues to suppress it.

BABEL Re-created

ANCIENT MAN — EXPLORING COMMONALITIES

As previously outlined in chapter 2, one of the main purposes of this book is to confirm biblical accounts of Genesis. Focusing on the divine creation of intelligent man and the effects of Babel and the dispersion, the following chapters will give evidences that verify the truth of the Bible. Because presupposition two and three are so interconnected, much of the data about ancient man supports both concepts. Indeed, there is so much data supporting these presuppositions that it is difficult to understand how people try to refute them! The majority of physical evidence in the world supports the intelligence of ancient man. As each new anomaly is studied and more out of place artifacts are found, it becomes increasingly clear that the explanations of evolution are becoming obsolete. On the other hand, the Bible is confirming itself as the only answer to life's big questions.

Similarly, the evidence authenticating the Tower of Babel and subsequent dispersion is phenomenal. As a recap: the evolutionary premise describes a slow process of discovery through trial and error through which civilizations and cultures sluggishly emerged. The biblical account is a direct contrast. Coming off the ark, Noah and his family would have had vast amounts of knowledge from their life before the Flood, and it would not take long for them to grow, expand, and create a new culture. Similarly, after dispersing from Babel, each new

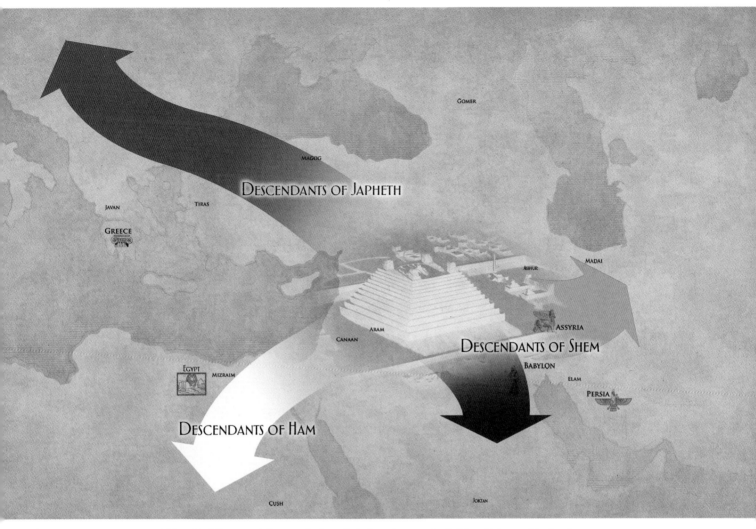

When God dispersed the people from Babel, each group took this religion and technology fully formed knowledge to their new locations.

tribe and nation would develop their own civilization rather quickly, building off of what they knew previously. Researcher Graham Hancock confirms that "the archeological evidence suggest[s] that rather than developing slowly and painfully . . . the civilization of Ancient Egypt, like that of the Olmecs, emerged all at once and fully formed."[1] Though it is likely that the dispersion decreased the diversity of technology and abilities in each of the new tribes, due to their connection at Babel they would all have similar characteristics in architecture, religion, and intelligence. All around the world these commonalities are seen in the different cultures, from similar legends to cultural practices to religious structures.

It is evident through the ruins of these ancient societies that they confirm the biblical account of Babel.

Throughout the following chapters, exciting data is presented that supports both the intelligence of ancient man and the dispersion at Babel. From speculations of pre-Flood man to evidence of worldwide travel, from advanced building techniques — common around the globe — to complex sciences and mathematics, prepare to be amazed at the accomplishments of ancient man. As you begin this section, try to lay down your preconceived ideas about history and rejoice as a whole new ancient world unfolds — one that rings with the truth of biblical records!

---

1   Hancock, *Fingerprints of the Gods*, p. 135.

chapter 5

*"As for Zillah, she also gave birth to Tubal-cain,
the forger of all implements of bronze and iron;
and the sister of Tubal-cain was Naamah."*

—*Genesis* 4:22

PRE-FLOOD MAN

The Bible describes the pre-Flood world very briefly from Genesis 1 through 6, so there is not much that can be stated as concrete fact. According to Genesis 4, the pre-Flood civilization had farms, livestock, music, cities, and tools, yet it is impossible to say how much technology they possessed. One would speculate that they had great abilities due to their close descent from Adam and Eve, the most intelligent humans created. Furthermore, this seemingly short section of the Bible encompasses over 1,500 years of civilization, giving early man generations to learn and advance. Oftentimes, people do not fully comprehend the length of time between creation and the Flood. Just think, the radio was invented in the late 1800s and in only a little over 100 years, technology has advanced to include automobiles, space shuttles, cellular phones, and the Internet. It would be foolish to assume that for over 1,500 years these people were unable to advance any further than Tubal-cain's bronze and iron forgery (Genesis 4:22).

Another interesting fact to keep in mind is the length of these ancient people's lives. Genesis 5 lists the descendants of Adam before the Flood of Noah, and interestingly gives the ages of the men who lived and died in those days. According to Scripture, men used to live for hundreds of years. For example, Adam lived to 930, Seth to 912, and Methuselah (the oldest man on record) to 969. Noah himself lived over 900 years. In a time when reaching one hundred years of age is considered out of the ordinary, it seems impossible for these numbers to be correct. Most would assume that human bodies just couldn't last that long. Yet interestingly, studies reveal that due to the constant production of new cells replacing old ones, the body is surprisingly self-sustaining.

The Bible makes it clear that people do not live as long as they used to. It is evident that the human body was created to last, designed to continually regenerate its cells. Perhaps the effects of the Curse have hindered the body's ability to continue this process inevitably. Modern studies show that the aging process is due to mutations and errors occurring in our body, especially at the microscopic level. There could be a number of factors, or combinations of effects, that could account for shorter life spans. Speculations of a more hospitable pre-Flood world could account for longer life spans as well as the fact that the generations closest to Adam and Eve would not suffer as much from the effects of the Curse as man does today. The drastic changes that occurred during the Flood certainly played a role in shortening the human life span, whether it was a difference in climate, a weaker magnetic field, a much smaller gene pool with post-Flood survivors, or the disintegrating ozone layer. Whatever the cause, men do not live as long as they used to and one has to speculate about what could be accomplished in a life spanning 900 years.

At first it may be hard to see the significance of these ages. The implications of such long lives combined with the superior intelligence of a human race not greatly affected by the Curse are fascinating to consider. To put things into perspective, one could use examples from history: what if Sir Isaac Newton had lived long enough to completely develop his theory of physics? Moreover, what if he had lived and worked with Albert Einstein? Think of the possibilities that blossom with the opportunity of geniuses living for hundreds of years! What about dynamic world leaders or powerful war strategists? What terror and destruction could atomic scientists come up with? Or imagine the beauty that could exist if artists and musicians had more time to explore their ideas and gifts? With such things in mind, it is not hard to fathom how Noah, after living 500 years, gaining wisdom and knowledge from others, perhaps working multiple careers, was able to build the ark, a massive engineering masterpiece. With so much time, each man could have spent years discovering, inventing, and sharing information, and developing advanced science, mathematics, astronomy, etc.

People often believe themselves to be part of the most advanced civilization yet to inhabit this earth. This secular viewpoint influences culture and education. In turn, the education system supports the view, as students are taught the steady progress of technology from the wheel in ancient Mesopotamia, to the telescope in the 17th century, to the video games of today. Therefore, it is not hard to understand why people evolutionarily assume that man has advanced to a height of intelligence beyond anything ever before. Yet what if this was not the case? As Ken Ham puts it, "When God created Adam, he was perfect. Today, the individual human intellect has suffered from 6,000 years of sin and decay. The sudden rise in technology in the last few centuries has nothing to do with increasing intelligence. . . . One of the most recent tools is the computer, which compensates a great deal for our natural decline in mental performance and discipline."[1] Getting away from an evolutionary mindset is difficult, but it influences the way that you view evidence. If you start with barbaric animal-like men evolving slowly, you would expect to find primitive civilizations slowly advancing into the complex technological civilization of today. If you start with extreme intelligence followed by decay, then you would expect to find evidence of advanced civilization right from the beginning with less impressive cultures and societies emerging from the original. This is more or less what is found.

Of course, the effects of the Flood cannot be ignored. Two thousand years of advancement was all but destroyed. Wiping out almost the entire world population, along with any records and evidence of their abilities, would have severely reduced the technology and development of civilization. There is no doubt that much of pre-Flood man's discoveries and information was lost at this time. Though Noah may have been able to preserve some things, how much was lost due to the flood will never be certain. Throughout history, the loss of ancient records due to various types of destruction and erosion is the frustration of every historian because it leaves so many holes. As such, one can only speculate about pre-Flood times and so, as fascinating as it is, this book will not focus on conjecture about pre-Flood man. Instead, it will outline post-Flood history and the intelligence that is evident since then.

Four Reasons for Little Information about the Pre-Flood World

1. Lost Knowledge of the Ancients

"Several events, both in ancient and modern times, have conspired to plunge the history of ancient nations into darkness. Those events have cast a veil of obscurity over such parts, as have reached our times, and have unfortunately bored others in oblivion. In the first class of those events, may be ranked the destruction of libraries. The famous library of Alexandria, founded by Ptolemy Philadelphus, about 284 years before the Christian era, consisted of vast collections of records, histories, tracts, poems, and works of taste. This immense repository of ancient science had been missing for several centuries. Here was amassed everything that was curious, valuable or elegant, among literary productions, since the days of Memnon, including, doubtless, all the ancient tales and genealogies, handed down by oral tradition before the invention of letters. This library was destroyed in the burning of Alexandria, by Julius Caesar.

Here were doubtless many valuable originals utterly lost. Before the art of printing, and especially in ancient times, there were but few books in the world; no work of magnitude could be obtained, but at a great expense. The Alexandrian library might have comprised half the books in the world, and very many of them with scarcely a duplicate existing. The loss was reckoned at 400,000 volumes. The institution was, however, revived, and a still greater collection made, which was enriched by the noble productions of the Augustan age. This flourished till the seventh century of the Christian era, when it was burned by the Saracens, who used the books for common fuel. There perished 700,000 volumes." (*A Compend of History* by Samuel Whelpley, A.M.; pages 28-29 (Boston: Richardson & Lord, 1822)

---

1   Ken Ham, *The New Answers Book 1*, Chapter 10, page 127, second full paragraph (Green Forest, AR: Master Books, 2006)

2. Inaccurate Assumptions Using Evolutionary Premises

For many people, it is simply self-evident that the earliest human beings had a low I.Q. because an evolutionary view of things demands that this be so. But if we follow Lyell's dictum of interpreting the past only in the light of the known present, it can be shown that most of the available evidence stands squarely against the current view of early man's lack of intelligence. There is absolutely no historical record of any primitive culture whose children were so lacking in intelligence that they could not hold their own with the children of civilized parents, when provided with comparable opportunities. Thus, although it is felt by many people that our primitive contemporaries are backward enough to be our contemporary ancestors, it is also important to underscore at the same time the well-recognized fact that our own newborn babies are not essentially different from those of any other culture, advanced or backward. Man seems always to start with about the same intellectual endowment regardless of whether he happens to be a member of some primitive tribe or a member of some well-to-do European family where it may be presumed opportunity for intellectual development is very high. It is opportunity that makes the difference. The apparent backwardness of some modern native cultures and the extreme simplicity of the tools and artifacts of Paleolithic Man are not, in either case, evidence of inferior intelligence but more probably due to a historical circumstance which it is well worth examining.

If this can be established, an important argument in favor of the supposed evolution of man from some animal form is weakened. And the object of this essay is simply to examine the evidence in the light of present knowledge. How intelligent was Paleolithic Man? (from "Part III: Establishing a Paleolithic I.Q.," Genesis and Early Man, Arthur Custance)

3. Overwhelming Focus of a Sinful Nature

Adam continued alive near two-thirds of the time before the flood; so that a very great part of those who were alive till the flood, might have opportunity of seeing and conversing with him, and hearing from his mouth, not only an account of his fall, and the introduction of the awful consequences of it, but also of his first finding himself in existence in the new-created world, of the creation of Eve, and what passed between him and his Creator in paradise.

But what was the success of these great means, to restrain men from sin, and to induce them to virtue? Did they prove sufficient? — instead of this, the world soon grew exceeding corrupt; till, to use our author's own words, mankind were universally debauched into lust, sensuality, rapine, and injustice.

~Jonathan Edwards (*The Great Christian Doctrine of Original Sin Defended*, Part 1 Chapter 1 Section VIII)

4. Destruction by the Global Flood

Evolutionary archaeologists have attempted to organize human history in terms of various supposed "ages"—Stone Age, Bronze Age, Iron Age, etc. The Noahic record, however, indicates that early men were very competent in brass and iron metallurgy, as well as agriculture, animal husbandry, and urbanization. It is significant that many kinds of bronze and iron implements are known to have been used in the earliest civilizations of Sumeria and Egypt. The same is true of musical instruments, and it is evident that the science and art of both metallurgy and music, as well as agriculture and animal husbandry, had been handed down from ancient times to these earliest post-flood civilizations. Modern archaeology is confirming the high degree of technology associated with the earliest human settlers all over the world. (*The Henry Morris Study Bible,* Green Forest, AR: Master Books, page 28)

The purpose of the flood—to destroy all flesh— could only have been accomplished by a worldwide deluge. The idea of a local flood is merely a frivolous conceit of Christians seeking to avoid imagined geological difficulties. Although many marine organisms would perish in the upheavals, everything in the earth (that is, "on the land") would die (ibid). The Bible does not disallow this as being grounds for information.

The amazing
symmetry of
Ramses II.

ADVANCED TECHNOLOGY

With an increased study of ancient cultures comes an increasing amount of surprise at what they may have known and been able to do. Many ancient cultures had developed a level of advancement in sciences and mathematics that modern scholars refuse to acknowledge. Not only is their technology fascinating, but also the undeniable similarities in the ancient technology around the world are intriguing. Charles Hapgood supports this, saying, "There are curious connections and comparisons that can be made between the ancient sciences of Greece, Egypt, Babylonia, and China."[1] This chapter will focus on some of the phenomenal evidences of this ancient advanced technology. From astronomy and timekeeping to building and irrigation, the people of ancient times were able to do much more than present-day historians give them credit for.

Science, man's pursuit of knowledge of the physical world, has been practiced since the most ancient of times. Mankind is fascinated with the world and in a constant state of search and discovery. In ancient times, with such long lives and intelligent minds, the people could have made discoveries and advancements that present-day man does not yet understand. Yet this knowledge they may have had has been mysteriously forgotten in most cases. Interestingly, Andrew Tomas, in his book *We Are Not the First,* makes one very significant note. "History shows that the priests of India, Sumer, Babylon, and Egypt as well as their confreres on the other side of the Atlantic — in Mexico and Peru — were custodians of science."[2] It could be that science and religion were intimately connected, allowing only the elite to possess certain knowledge. Unfortunately, this would have made it easier for the knowledge to be lost or confused in transmission through the generations. This could have played a role in the loss of advanced technology until more present times.

The intricate frontispiece of the Diamond Sutra from Tang Dynasty China, 868 AD (British Museum).

Some brief examples of advanced science include the chemistry of the Egyptians in making cosmetics and pigment. The ancient chemists were able to manufacture artificial lead-based compounds and add them to the cosmetics! The ancient Greeks had working steam boilers, and in Egypt there were "slot-machines" for holy water! The Chinese are well known for their ancient technology, credited with the invention of movable type (A.D. 1045), writing paper, the seismograph (A.D. 132), and the first mechanical clock (A.D. 725). Still another example of ancient intelligence is found in the statues of Ramses II. They are all perfectly symmetrical and under computer analysis it is evident that the builders used the Pythagorean triangle and the Golden triangle in the architecture. This amazing symmetry has scholars debating whether the Egyptians may have given Pythagoras his triangle concepts. These are just a few examples of the great scientific advancements that were present in ancient times.

ASTRONOMY

Starting at Babel, astronomy has almost always been connected to the ancient religions of the post-Flood world. (The ancient people's fascination with the heavens lends further support to the idea of priest-scientists.) It is clear that that they

---

1   Hapgood, *Maps of the Ancient Sea Kings* (Kempton, IL: Adventures Unlimited Press, 1966, new edition 1996), p.185.
2   Andres Tomas, *We Are Not the First.* (Souvenir Press Ltd., 1971), p.124.

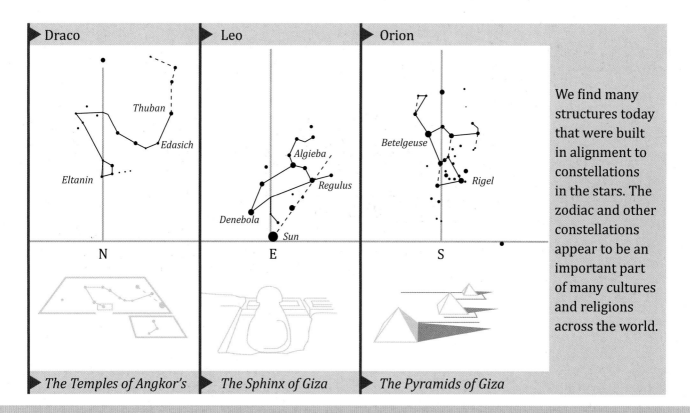

Draco

Thuban

Edasich

Eltanin

N

Leo

Algieba

Regulus

Denebola

Sun

E

Orion

Betelgeuse

Rigel

S

We find many structures today that were built in alignment to constellations in the stars. The zodiac and other constellations appear to be an important part of many cultures and religions across the world.

▶ *The Temples of Angkor's* ▶ *The Sphinx of Giza* ▶ *The Pyramids of Giza*

were skilled in astronomical studies and greatly interested in astrological signs. They used the stars practically, for time-keeping and travel, as well as religiously, aligning their monuments and buildings to different heavenly phenomena and constellations. Indeed, the zodiac and other constellations appear to be an important part of many cultures.

The Greeks and Babylonians are credited with the invention of the zodiac that is popular today, yet there are some interesting characteristics of the zodiac that imply they were not the first ones to use it. The Graeco-Babylonian zodiac includes all 12 signs, but only 4 of the signs have any real significance at a time: signifying the spring and autumn equinoxes and the winter and summer solstices. (The signs change due to precession movement.) Today these four are Pisces, Virgo, Gemini, and Sagittarius, but at the time of the Greeks and Babylonians (around the second millennia B.C.), they would have been Aries, Libra, Cancer, and Capricorn. Therefore, it seems odd that they would have included all the others. For all the signs to have significance, one must go back into the past to at least the year 4400 B.C. The implication is that the Babylonians and Greeks must have gotten their zodiac

as a legacy from some earlier source. Furthermore, this earlier source could have influenced other cultures around the world as well, explaining why the same constellations are so universal. Indeed, the striking similarity between the Western zodiac and that of the pre-Columbian Maya indicates the two cultures must have had the same source.

There are some astonishing examples of an ancient sophisticated knowledge of the universe. Accurate charts and perfectly aligned monuments testify to careful study of the night sky. There is even evidence from many structures to show that ancient man had the advanced knowledge of

Mayan Calendar

astronomical movements, including the process of precession. (Precession is the minute shifting of the constellations as the earth wobbles in its spin, approximately 1 degree per 72 years.) Even in their legends, they use numbers indicating knowledge of precession and many of their structures are aligned with these movements in mind. Researcher James Nienhuis, author of *Ice Age Civilizations,* describes how these numbers and this precession knowledge is found everywhere in the cultures and legends of the ancient peoples. He brings this a step further and says that with it they were able to easily travel and accurately map the globe. Further evidence of advanced astronomy is evident in the worship of Sirius A and B, binary stars. Both the Dogon people of Africa as well as the Egyptians and Babylonians worshiped these two stars, which from the naked eye seem to be only one star.

Knowledge of the binary stars as well as early records of the rings of Saturn cause many to believe that the early people used telescope-like lenses in their observations of the heavens. The ancient use of lenses is evidenced by several other proofs. Childress claims that, for the most part, archaeologists agree that glass and crystal lenses were present in the ancient cultures and they also had relatively sophisticated glass technology. Most were made of rock crystal until the fourth century B.C. when glass lenses became available. In fact, at least 450 lenses have been found, used for different purposes ranging from fire starting to carving microscopic engravings. The Viking sun-stone is a form of lens that is supposed to have helped the ancient people navigate by finding the sun on a cloudy day.

Ancient people also used the heavens for timekeeping. Cultures all around the globe had calendars based on the sun, moon, and stars. The famous Mayan calendar, which some suggest they got from people prior to them, is a great example of ancient and accurate timekeeping. Consisting of a complex three-calendar system, the Mayans had a 365-day year, yet they knew that the year was actually a little longer. Their estimate of 365.242036 is actually more accurate than the Gregorian calendar that is currently used worldwide!

The Antikythera Mechanism is dated at least 2,000 years old – created ahead of modern-day technology!

An extremely advanced and perplexing artifact that charted the heavens and kept time is the Antikythera Mechanism (picture). Found in 1900 in the wreckage from a second-century B.C. Roman merchant ship, it is probably the most scientifically advanced artifact of the ancient world. The mechanism, about the size of a shoebox, is believed to be a mechanical computing device, at least 2,000 years old. Thirty of its original bronze gears are still intact, with the total number suggested to be 37. It is extremely complex, able to predict the movements of the sun, moon, the 12 signs of the zodiac, and possibly the five planets then known to the Greeks. It tracked the Saros, Metonic, and Callippic cycles. Apparently, it also tracked the four-year cycle of the Olympic games so the people would know which games were being played in each year. It wasn't until 17th-century clocks that anything in comparison was made.

Clearly, even in ancient times, people knew of the importance of the heavens. They were curious about the universe just as people are today, and were aptly capable of successful study and using their discoveries to their advantage. This fascination with the heavens is natural, for God said in Genesis 1:14 that the "lights in the expanse" were for "signs and for seasons and for days and years." Furthermore, God "counts the number of the stars [and] He gives names to all of them" (Psalm 147:4), so perhaps man too has the desire to know the stars as God does (see chapter 4 for more on stars).

ARCHITECTURE

More evidence of ancient man's intelligence comes from the architecture and construction of their structures. Not only are there similar styles seen around the world, but there is also a puzzling lack of tools around these amazingly advanced buildings. This leaves researchers scrambling to theorize how the builders created such fascinating monuments. Many of the impressive buildings are made up of huge stones, with very little evidence testifying to how the ancient people fitted them into place. Such megalithic stones can be found all over, from the pyramids of Egypt to the stone circles of Britain to the Moai of Easter Island in the middle of the Pacific Ocean. Many unexplainable examples found in Peru have odd polygon shapes fitted precisely together like puzzle pieces with no mortar in between. Still more interestingly, many underwater cities have been discovered with the same megalithic construction. (See chapter 8 and 12).

Most of these megalithic projects are thought to have been completed around the same time, commonly dated to around 2000 B.C. Experts are baffled that thousands of years after construction the joints are still precise and the cracks haven't weathered but, rather, have possibly become a better fit. Currently, most of the cracks are so thin that you can't slide a credit card into them. The structures are so stable, in fact, that people throughout history have built upon them because they have passed the test of time. Yet, even with so many well-preserved examples to study, scientists have not found a way to explain how the ancients accomplished such feats. Of course, working from an evolutionary time-line, the level of technology and skill needed doesn't fit their paradigm, therefore making the construction very difficult to explain. However, with the starting point that man was created highly intelligent, one can theorize that the ancient people may have had advanced technology and abilities that don't exist today.

Scrambling for an explanation, there are many theories as to how the structures were built, but each has very little support. There are no depictions of cranes or other pulley systems which could have been used, nor are there examples of advanced machinery. With only a few vague drawings and ancient legends, it's close to impossible to come to a concrete solution. Theories range from the physically draining and impractically large labor forces pulling blocks into place (based on depictions in Egyptian hieroglyphs) to the fantastic legends of builders being able to float the huge stones by whistling or humming. Theories include:

▸ Dinosaurs and/or other animals were domesticated and could have been used for their strength.

- A system of ramps, scaffolding, cranes, and pulleys was used.

- Men carried liquid "cement" and the blocks were actually poured and shaped in forms.

- There may have been some natural chemical that softened the stone to make its contours more workable.

- Men used levitation to lift, transport, and place the stones.

- Giants helped build structures.

- Half-demon or demon-possessed people with increased strength aided the builders.

Some of the options seem outlandish or unrealistic, but this only serves to confirm the mystery of the whole issue. Most people can quickly denounce any of the above suggestions, yet when asked to come up with their own, it seems impossible. Still, each of the options has some possibility.

For instance, the study of electrogravitics and acoustic levitation is becoming highly popular. Donald Chittick, in The Puzzle of Ancient Man, explains that electrogravitics have been used in the developments of the B-2 bomber, so it could be a real possibility. Mysteries such as the coral castle in Florida, supported by ancient legends of levitation, leave the possibility that anti-gravity could be achieved using certain frequencies of sound. Chittick also explains how the logistics of building these megaliths make traditional building techniques unlikely or at least very difficult. Furthermore, the various accounts of levitation throughout history add more confirmation to this theory. David Hatcher Childress points out that the Catholic Church claims to have two hundred saints able to conquer the force of gravity. So perhaps the supernatural was involved somehow. One must always keep in mind that Satan, who instigated the building of the very first tower, has abilities and powers that he would not fear to implement if it meant further perverting God's plan. Again, one has to wonder how much the supernatural (good or evil) may have helped accomplish some of these immense buildings and structures. It is not out of the question that the ancient people not only had advanced technology, but also aid from supernatural forces.

Yet there is also evidence that other less mystical efforts were employed. Christopher Dunn, a master craftsman and skilled machinist, has done extensive hands-on research on the pyramids of Egypt and he points to evidence of machine-worked artifacts as well as that of high-velocity drills, saws, and industrial-quality lathes. Much of his findings show techniques that have only recently been discovered.

Monte Albán, Mexico. One of the earliest cities in Mesoamerica, the site still contains a large plaza, large platforms with impressive staircases, and carved monuments.

Precise stonework, Valley Temple of Khafre, Egypt. Some blocks weigh over 100 metric tons.

Both larger and smaller cuts and drill holes - Puma Punku, Bolivia.

Another researcher, Sir Flinders Petrie, who died in the middle of the 20th century, spent his whole life studying Egypt and tools. He discovered that diamonds would have been needed for the drilling work evidenced on Egyptian artifacts, but none were ever found in Egypt. Dunn gives further credence to this theory by Petrie and sees evidence for silicon-carbide looped wires that are currently used for cutting granite and other hard rocks. However, though copper was known and used by Egyptians, it is too soft to be used to chisel hard rock like granite. There are many examples of fine (fast) drill marks, saw marks, polished surfaces, extremely flat surfaces, and intricate 3-D contouring that so far have no explanation. Where the Egyptians got their diamonds and other materials for tools is still unknown and the disappearance of said tools makes the mystery even greater.

These straight cuts and drill holes are found in other places, too, such as in Puma Punku, Bolivia.

Puma Punku shows the results of highly advanced stone-cutting techniques. Many of the blocks strewn about the Puma Punku area are intricately cut and shaped so that they fit together like Lego pieces. Experienced stone sculptor Roger Hopkins verifies the difficulty of the precision inner cuts and inner boxes that are cut into the blocks, claiming that it would be difficult even with our modern equipment to get that type of precision. He explains how these carvings would normally be done with robotic arms following computer patterns, yet still don't turn out accurate sometimes. This causes some researchers to wonder if the ancient people were able to soften the rock and shape it or if they poured rocks like concrete. However, the composition does not suggest a type of man-made concrete. Interestingly, the people who built Puma Punku are not even credited with having knowledge of the wheel or a system of writing, yet the construction of these blocks would have required a high level of engineering and mathematics.

Another example of advanced building techniques and creativity is found in South America and Egypt. Both ancient cultures used metal clamps in their

Sites like Puma Punku confound researchers because they are evidence of high levels of engineering, mathematics, and precise construction, like building blocks (top left), complex-shaped blind holes (top right) or I-shaped metal clamps (below).

blocks to hold them together. They would melt the metal and pour it into spaces between the blocks so that when it hardened it held the blocks together. This indicates that the ancient people had the knowledge and ability of smelting, confirming Genesis 4:22 which records that Tubal-cain was a forger.

Still, the utter lack of the tools themselves casts doubt on the idea that the ancients used such advanced machinery. It seems odd that there is no record or remains of them. Some suggest the people would have destroyed or re-used metals captured from other people groups, or the tools could have deteriorated or rusted to nothing through the ages. Still others point out that the tools may have been expensive and rare or perhaps only operated by the elite or religious groups. However, even with these explanations and apparent evidence of power tools, the option is far from being heralded as the ultimate solution.

How the magnificent buildings and monuments were constructed may never be known. How much knowledge and abilities these ancient builders possessed may always be a mystery to the modern world.

SANITATION & IRRIGATION

Another interesting proof of advancement and intelligence is the ancient sanitation and irrigation systems. In the book *Technology of the Gods,* David Hatcher Childress lists many examples of ancient plumbing and irrigation, such as the walls and terraces that the Nabatean people built to utilize the small amount of rainfall. Childress also explains how ancient Persians, 3,000 years ago, built underground aqueducts to bring mountain ground water to the dry plains. Today, their ancient system is still functioning and supplying Iran with 75 percent of its water!

Ancient Tell Asmar near Baghdad had household plumbing in some houses as well as temples. At Tell el-Amarna, an "elaborate bath" was discovered; apparently many of the ancient bathrooms were very luxurious, just as they are today. Childress also shares how the Egyptians knew how to make drains of copper — one found was 450 yards long. The people of the ancient Indus Valley civilization are credited with the world's first urban sanitation system. Their sewage and drainage systems were far more advanced than contemporary sites in the Middle East and even

Aqueduct in an archaeological dig, Israel.

Ancient Harrapa, Pakistan –
The Indus Valley Civilization
is known for cities displaying
planned layouts, wide
streets, water management, and
sanitation: reservoirs, drains, personal
and public wells and bathing platforms.

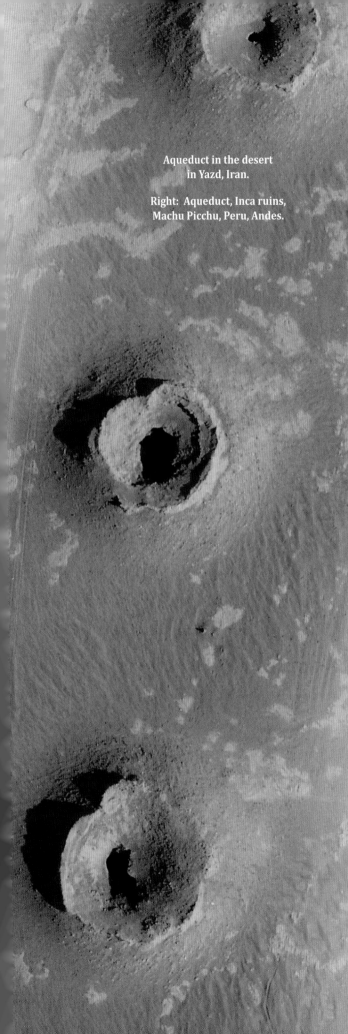

Aqueduct in the desert
in Yazd, Iran.

Right: Aqueduct, Inca ruins,
Machu Picchu, Peru, Andes.

more efficient than those used in India today. There are even a couple of bigger projects, such as the Sri Lankan dam at Maduru Oya and the dam at Marib in Yemen. Also, many ancient civilizations built terraces on the sides of hills and mountains to increase the amount of cropland available and regulate water from the mountain springs or reservoirs. This was and is popular in Asia where complex and regimented social structures are imperative in order for the system to work. In South America, the Incas are also known for their beautiful terraced hillsides. Ancient man knew how to use water and how to keep himself clean and sanitary. Some say, "The mark of any advanced civilization is the level of their sanitation and plumbing."

Ancient man's advanced technology can be clearly seen in what they have left behind. Whether it be accurate time-keeping and calendars or the megalithic structures that have no explanation, it is obvious that the secular mindset of the modern world has greatly underestimated the people of the past.

chapter 7

"*Therefore its name is called Babel, because there the LORD confused the language of the whole earth; and from there the LORD scattered them abroad over the face of the whole earth.*"

—*Genesis 11:9*

WORLDWIDE TRAVEL

At the dispersion of Babel, mankind spread around the globe, populating the continents and starting new civilizations. There is debate about how people first arrived in places like the Americas or Australia. Did they travel over land bridges during the Ice Age? Were they advanced enough to travel by boat across the sea? Remember that Noah and his sons were experienced ship builders and they lived for some time after the Flood. It is likely that they would have passed on their knowledge and perhaps have built their own boats. It is not impossible for ancient man to have traveled the seas with ease in their time.

Almost without exception, each child is taught that Christopher Columbus discovered the New World. Yet even mainstream scientists and historians agree that the Vikings were actually the first to discover and settle in America (not to mention the native peoples already living there!) in the late tenth century. However, there are many theories and evidences that point to "discovery" far earlier than that.

ANOMALIES

From the Phoenicians to the Chinese to the Romans, there are theories of contact in the Americas far earlier than commonly believed. Jonathan Gray, in his article "Solomon's Fleet Mystery," describes evidence of Phoenicians, claiming they left inscriptions in North America and Brazil. Gray suggests that King Solomon's fleets may have been getting their gold and silver from a more distant destination than commonly assumed. He states that Columbus supposedly found large ancient mines in Hispaniola that could have been the source.[1] Gray even defends the Phoenician's possible influence in the Pacific islands by the similarities in the linguistics of Phoenicians, Samoans, those of Tahiti, and many more. Others claim that the Chinese were in America in ancient times and even influenced the Olmec culture.[2] There are still more who assert that Egyptians, Japanese, and Romans visited the Americas as well.[3] Still, it is surmised that the Phoenicians had the corner on the market and possibly spread the myth of hazardous ocean travel and the danger of sailing off the edge of the earth.

Interestingly, there are traditions elsewhere in the world that describe sea travel. In Cambodia, the people believe that their civilization was founded by two demi-gods who came by boat across the sea. Similarly, the Mayans claim that their leader, Itzamna, brought them across the water. Also, there are legends about Easter Island, declaring it was first inhabited by a group of 300 survivors of a "great cataclysm" who sailed there in two very large canoes. Indeed, the very existence of the ancient civilization on Easter Island (in the middle of the Pacific Ocean) requires advanced ancient sea travel.

Researcher William Corliss has made it part of his life's work to record many of the anomalies and out-of-place artifacts that are found and documented that don't seem to fit the current paradigm. Corliss's extensive research and bookkeeping provides lists of these anomalies, forcing a re-evaluation of the theory. Things that don't belong, such as potatoes in Oceana, Old World shells in the New World, Egyptian coins in Australia, Hebrew coins in North America, and countless others, testify to the fact that man has been moving around the world for some time.[4]

There are many traditions, legends, and accounts of people with European features in the Americas. For example, the Quetzalcoatl cult is based around a god who is described as a tall white man with yellow hair and a beard. Viracocha, the "Bearded White God" of some South American cultures, is another proof that people claim as evidence of contact. The "Kennewick Man" is the name of

---

1   Jonathan Gray, "Solomon's Fleet Mystery," accessed April 15, 2011, http://www.beforeus.com/email/article/art2_solfleet.html.

2   "Shang in America," The Jade Road, accessed April 15, 2011, http://www.thejaderoad.com/america.html.

3   "Pre-Columbian Trans-oceanic Contact," Wikipedia, accessed April 15, 2011, http://en.wikipedia.org/wiki/Pre-Columbian_trans-oceanic_contact#cite_note-The_Mystery_of_the_Cocaine_Mummies-14.

4   William Corliss, "Archeology," Science Frontiers, accessed April 14, 2011, http://www.science-frontiers.com/cat-arch.htm.

57

a skeleton found in Washington State that supposedly dates back 9,000 years. Found on the banks of the Kennewick River, the skeleton has European features unlike any of the Native Americans of the area. There is also evidence of ancient Egyptians in North America. There are rumors of an Egyptian settlement in the Grand Canyon, and Burrow's Cave in Illinois was said to contain Egyptian artifacts buried in the silt, thought to be 2,700 years old. The copper mines found in upper Wisconsin are believed to be supposedly 5,000 years old and some suggest the Mediterranean peoples used them during their bronze age.

MAPS

Charles Hapgood, in his book *Maps of the Ancient Sea Kings,* relates his investigation of surprisingly advanced medieval maps. He discovered that there is evidence that these maps were based on much older, yet accurate maps. The medieval maps encompass great regions including the Americas, Antarctica, and Africa, with surprising accuracy in longitude and latitude. The depictions of Antarctica are perhaps most stunning because the continent wasn't officially discovered until 1820,[5] much later than the creation of the maps. Some maps apparently depict the continent's shape and features accurately. These include the Piri Reis map of 1513 as well as the Oronteus Finaeus map of 1531.

Some claim that the Piri Reis map appears to show the Antarctica coastline without its ice cap (this is highly debated) as well as parts of Africa, the Gulf of Mexico, and the coast of South America. Piri Reis sources nearly 20 earlier maps that he compiled to make his. Despite its errors (most likely due to copying from other maps), researchers who have studied it can testify to the advanced mathematics and knowledge involved in the projection of this map and its possible source maps.[6] The Oronteus Finaeus map shows Antarctica with mountains and rivers, signifying that it was created with knowledge

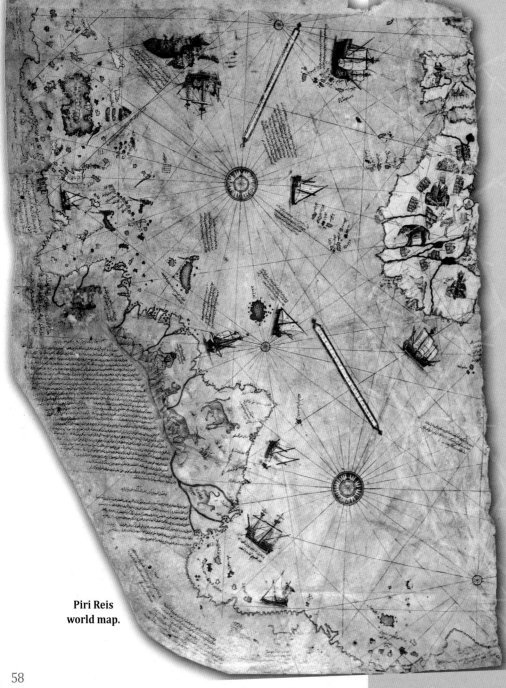

Piri Reis world map.

5   "Who Discovered Antarctica," Who Discovered It, accessed April 13, 2011, http://www.whodiscoveredit.com/who-discovered-antarctica.html.
6   Hapgood, *Maps of the Ancient Sea Kings.* Also see Jonathan Crowe, "The Piri Reis Map of 1513," The Map Room, February 1, 2007, accessed April 14, 2011, http://www.maproomblog.com/2007/02/the_piri_reis_map_of_1513.php.

of the continent before the ice covered it. Yet some claim that it still follows the geography of Antarctica's coastline with ice. Still, the map points to a much earlier discovery of Antarctica than previously thought.[7] The accuracy of these maps and many others is especially significant because a consistent clock is needed in order to find longitude. In the modern era, we only achieved such a clock in 1761.[8]

However, some pose the theory that longitude could also be determined by using the ancient Celtic cross. The familiar cross, seen adorning gravesides and churches, is thought to be the Mayan's lost "Staff of Power." With proper use of the cross, using simple angle measurement, one could supposedly "tell the time, find latitude and longitude, measure the angles of the stars, predict the solstices and equinoxes, and measure the precession of the equinoxes. The instrument can also find the ecliptic pole as well as the North and South poles, it can make maps and charts, design pyramids and henges and, when it is used in combination with . . . observatory sites, can record and predict the cycles of nature."[9] It then becomes evident that those who used such a tool would need a system of writing and record-keeping in order to experiment correctly and accurately understand these

concepts so that they could use them. If this advanced technique was used in creating these ancient maps and their source maps, the men who charted them had to be highly intelligent as well.

Another interesting fact is that there are more islands on the medieval maps than exist today. This could be consistent with the idea of Atlantis, Lemuria, and the hypothetical ancient island of Mu. Such islands would have been covered as the Ice Age came to an end and the ocean levels rose. If such is the case, it pushes the creation of the original source maps, and therefore their intelligent creators, back before 1600 B.C.

Artist's conception of lost city of Atlantis

7   Hapgood, *Maps of the Ancient Sea Kings*; Paul Heinrich, "The Mysterious Origins of Man: The Oronteus Finaeus Map of 1532," June 6, 1996, The TalkOrigins Archive, accessed April 14, 2011, http://www.talkorigins.org/faqs/mom/oronteus.html.
8   Dava Sobel, *Longitude: The True Story of a Lone Genius Who Solved the Greatest Scientific Problem of His Time,* (New York, NY: Penguin Books, 1995), p. 56–57.
9   Crichton E.M. Miller, "The Working Celtic Cross," accessed April 16, 2011, http://www.viewzone.com/crichton.html; Nienhuis, Ice Age Civilizations.

BOATS

Along with the advanced maps, there is evidence of advanced boat-making abilities across different cultures. Jonathan Gray claims the Phoenicians were advanced enough to have large, seaworthy commercial ships sailing all over the world, carrying up to 500 people, even in the time of King Solomon (circa 950 B.C.) and possibly before.[10] It is known that they had very large cargo ships, comparable in size to the one Columbus used, so this is not impossible. In fact, it is interesting that the Polynesians, who haven't been considered an especially advanced culture in today's terms, have been known to spread and control many island areas in the Pacific Ocean. They must have had incredibly advanced navigational techniques in order to explore, settle, and find their way back home on these journeys. It was thought that they used double hull boats such as the ones Captain Cook discovered in Tahiti, but after some experimenting, Robert Webb's Liki Tiki project proves this would have been impossible. He suggested the Polynesians used outrigger canoes instead, after proving their stability on a 5,000-mile journey from Panama to Hawaii. Also, the Egyptians developed different kinds of riverboats for travel up and down the Nile. A depiction of a sailboat supposedly dating back to 3200 B.C. verifies the antiquity of their skill. The Egyptians also used papyrus reeds to build boats similar to the ones used across the ocean in Peru. These boats are still used for fishing on Lake Titicaca today.[11]

There are also accounts and descriptions of very large ancient warships around the size of Noah's ark! Since the seventh century B.C., many navel battles were won and lost due to these huge ships, powered by 2–40 banks of oars. For instance, the 120–150 foot Leontifera fought in a battle on the Aegean Sea in 280 B.C. Even more impressive,

In the Qobustan Petroglyph Reserve there are more than 6,000 petroglyphs carved by the hunter-gatherers that lived in these caves thousands of years ago in what is now Azerbaijan. The petroglyph of this reed boat is similar to those depicted in cave paintings in Scandinavia, something that made researcher and adventurer Thor Heyerdahl theorise that the Scandinavians originally came from this area. Yet, across the ocean in Huanchaco, Peru, these reed fishing boats bear a remarkable resemblance to those of the petroglyphs.

10 Jonathan Gray, "Solomon's Fleet Mystery"; Thomas Crawford Johnston, *Did the Phoenicians Discover America?* (London: James Nisbet and Co., Ltd., 1913), p. 70–104, 289; Constance Irwin, Fair Gods and Stone Faces (London: W.H. Allen, 1964), p. 228–229, 235.

11 Ancient Egyptian Boats, http://www.kingtutshop.com/freeinfo/egyptian-boats.htm, accessed December 1, 2011.

From the writings of Pliny the Elder (AD 23–79), the table (below) references ships of antiquity. This documents the rapid advances the ancients made in ship-building technology in just a few centuries. The time period in the table is from about the seventh century BC to the end of the third century BC.[13]

Vessel	Inventor	Authority	Approx. Time
Double-banked galley	The Erythraeans	Damastes	7th C. B.C.
Trireme (three banks of oars)	Aminocles of Corinth	Thucydides	6th C. B.C.
Quadrireme (four banks)	The Carthaginians	Aristotle	5th C. B.C.
Quinquereme (five)	The Salaminians	Mnesigiton	4th C. B.C.
Galleys with six banks of oars	The Syracusans	Xenagoras	4th C. B.C.
Up to ten banks	Alexander the Great	Mnesigiton	4th C. B.C.
Up to twelve banks	Ptolemy Soter	Philostephanus	3rd C. B.C.
Up to fifteen banks	Demetrius, son of Antigonus	Philostephanus	3rd C. B.C.
Up to thirty banks	Ptolemy Philadelphus	Philostephanus	3rd C. B.C.
Up to forty banks	Ptolemy Philopator, surname Tryphon	Philostephanus	3rd C. B.C.

Ptolemy Philopator built a 420-foot-long warship around 200 B.C., which had a crew of 7, 250 men![12]

It is evident that people of ancient days had knowledge of the seas and how to get around on them. These ancient cultures were not isolated from each other. They were not afraid to venture out and discover, and they had the intelligence and ability to do so. God created man to rule the earth, and therefore one should expect such knowledge and skills to exist in the early times. It is only the evolutionary paradigm that has issues with the evidence of early worldwide travel.

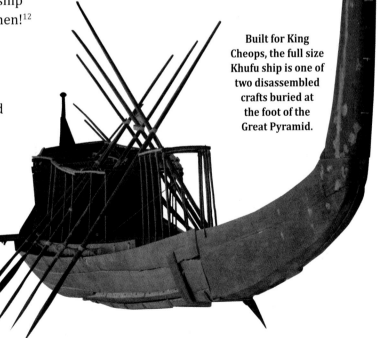

Built for King Cheops, the full size Khufu ship is one of two disassembled crafts buried at the foot of the Great Pyramid.

12 Larry Pierce, The Large Ships of Antiquity, http://www.answersingenesis.org/articles/cm/v22/n3/ships, accessed December 1, 2011.
13 Ibid.

chapter 8

Pyramids of Egypt - Mizraim is the name for ancient Upper and Lower Egypt; Mizraim is the son of Ham, one of Noah's three sons.

MONUMENTS, MOUNDS, PYRAMIDS . . .

The evidence of ancient man's intelligence can be seen in monuments and structures all over the world. These same buildings also testify to the dispersion at Babel due to their similar characteristics. There are pyramids, ziggurats, mounds, and stone circles spotting the globe. The fact that these structures are so common and their architecture is so similar directly links them to each other and the original Tower of Babel. In fact, in his book *Masks of God*, Joseph Campbell claims, "There is archaeological evidence supporting a direct link between Mesopotamian ziggurats and the pyramids of Egypt."[1] He goes on to show how people spread from these middle-eastern places and took their culture east, eventually to the Americas. In this chapter, many specific examples will be given which confirm both the intelligence of ancient man as well as the biblical record of the Tower of Babel.

The Great Pyramid of Giza is by far the most famous of megalithic ancient structures. Last of the "Seven Wonders of the Ancient World," it has held the fascination and awe of mankind for centuries. However, merely looking at it does not portray the real significance of the pyramid. Careful studies of the structure reveal characteristics of its construction that baffle archeologists. For instance, the pyramid is precisely aligned true north within 3/60 of a degree and its other three sides also directly face the cardinal directions. The base, covering 13 acres, is only 7/8" out of level. The steep angle of the sides, unique to the pyramids of Giza, is 51 degrees 51 minutes. The Great Pyramid and its two neighbors are also astronomically aligned precisely to the constellation Orion, each one representing a star in the stellar belt. How the ancient architects were able to achieve such precise measurements and alignments is yet to be determined. They also used a mortar, stronger than rock, to join the casing stones together — most with less than 1/50" between them. Add to this the problem of moving

over a million limestone blocks, averaging 2.5–15 tons each, with the largest about 80 tons, and the Great Pyramid of Giza becomes an even greater mystery. Contrary to what one would expect, later pyramids show much less precision and skill. They are greatly inferior to these early ones.

The symbols on the two-sided Phaistos Disk from the Minoan palace of Phaistos on the Greek island of Crete remains a undeciphered mystery.

Though Egypt is most famous for its pyramids, these amazing structures can be seen around the world, signifying that they originated from Babel. The Pyramid of the Sun in Mexico actually contains many surprising similarities to the Great Pyramid, including very similar perimeter dimensions. Mexico has many other pyramids, including the Pyramid of the Magician in Uxmal and the Pyramid of Kukulkan at Chichen Itza, most of them astronomically aligned. The pyramids in Mexico, many connected with the cult of Quetzalcoatl, were seen as "portals to the otherworld," just as Giza is known to the Egyptians as the "Gateway to the Otherworld."

1   "Ziggurat," accessed May 4, 2011, http://www.crystalinks.com/ ziggurat.html; Joseph Campbell, *Creative Mythology, Vol. 4: The Masks of Gods* (New York: Penguin Group, USA, Inc., 1991).

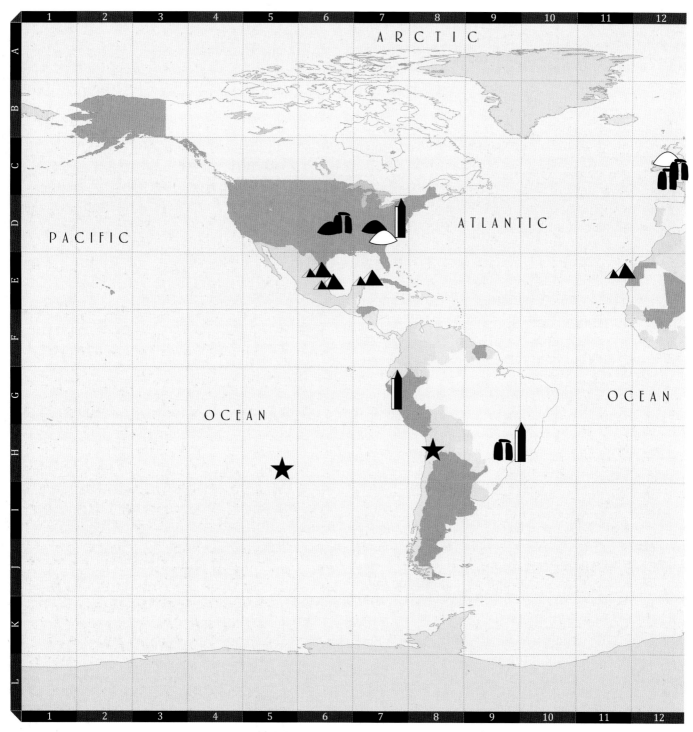

ARCTIC

PACIFIC

ATLANTIC

OCEAN

OCEAN

 Pyramids:

D15   Great Pyramid of Giza (Egypt)

E7   Pyramid of Kukulkan (Mexico)

E6   Pyramid of the Sun (Mexico)

E6   Pyramid of the Magician (Mexico)

D20   White Pyramid (China)

D13   Pyramids of Montevecchia (Italy)

E11   Pyramids of Guimar (Canary Islands/Spain)

E15   Royal Pyramids of Nubia (Sudan)

D14   Pyramids of Argolis (Greece)

Ziggurats:

D15   Boraippa Ziggurat (Iraq)

D16   White Temple of Uruk ziggurat (Iraq)

E16   Etemenanki or Marduk Ziggurat (Iraq)

D15   Ziggurat of Dur-Kurigalzu (Iraq)

E16   Chogha Zanbil ziggurat (Iran)

D16   Sialk ziggurat (Iran)

Stele/Obelisks:

D7   Washington Monument obelisk (U.S.)

G7   Raimondi Stela (Peru)

E15   Temple of Luxor obelisk
      (Egypt; second in France)

F15   King Ezana's Stele (Sudan)

D14   Obelisk of Tuthmosis III (Turkey)

D13   Obelisks of Beneveto (Italy)

F18   Keralian Obelisk (India)

D13   Arles Obelisk (France)

E15   Obelisk of Herod the Great (Israel)

H9   San Paulo obelisk (Brazil)

Egyptian obelisks have also been found in
Egypt, France, Italy, Turkey, Poland, and Israel. Assyrians also made obelisks, and there
are a number of steles from Ethiopia.

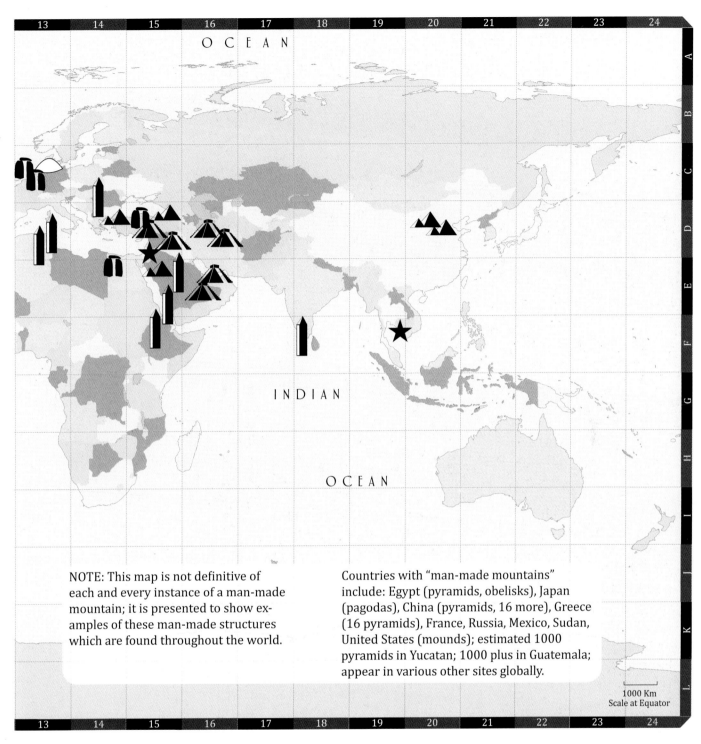

NOTE: This map is not definitive of each and every instance of a man-made mountain; it is presented to show examples of these man-made structures which are found throughout the world.

Countries with "man-made mountains" include: Egypt (pyramids, obelisks), Japan (pagodas), China (pyramids, 16 more), Greece (16 pyramids), France, Russia, Mexico, Sudan, United States (mounds); estimated 1000 pyramids in Yucatan; 1000 plus in Guatemala; appear in various other sites globally.

1000 Km
Scale at Equator

Mounds:

D6   Monk's Mound (U.S.)

D7   Serpent Mound State Park (U.S.)

Effigy Mounds (internationally):

D7   Serpent Mounds Park (Canada)

C12   Loch Nell Serpent Mound in (Scotland)

C13   Rotherwas Serpent Mound (U.K.)

(For more information on mounds in the U.S. please see the map on page 68.)

Henges:

C12   Stonehenge (U.K.)

D15   Gilgal Refaim Henge (Israel)

C13   Ales Stenar (ship-shaped henge; Sweden)

E14   Nabta Henge (Egypt)

H9   Brazil's Stone Henge (Amazon/Brazil)

D6   Woodhenge, west of Monks
Mound in   Cahokia (U.S.)

C12   Woodhenge (Amesbury, U.K.)

C13   Wood Henge (Netherlands)

Henges can also be found in Britain (over 900), Sweden, Armenia, United States, and Egypt.

Important sites include:

H8   Puma Punku/Tiwanaku (Bolivia)

D15   Baalbek (Lebanon)

F19   Angkor Wat (Cambodia)

H5   Easter Island or Rapa Nui (Chile)

Chinese pyramids are ancient mausoleums — tomb of Emperor Jing of Han.

Bosnian "pyramids" remain controversial.

In China, though reports were first denied, a series of 16 pyramids, also astronomically aligned, has been confirmed. Some archeologists believe there could be up to one hundred pyramids in China, with the legendary White Pyramid rumored to be 1,000 feet tall! In Bosnia there is an ongoing debate about whether Visocica Hill is a man-made pyramid or a natural formation. If man-made, it would be the largest in the world.

Near Milan, in Italy, there are three pyramid-shaped hills that are aligned with Orion's passing on the summer solstice. The area is known as the Italian Gizeh. There are 16 documented pyramids in Greece and in France there is one about 30 feet (9 meters) tall near Nice. Even in Russia, near the city of Vladivostok, two suspicious twin hills are reputed to be gigantic stone pyramids. On the African island of Mauritius, there have been seven pyramids identified. These are paralleled with pyramids found on the island Tenerife, on the opposite side of the continent!

Sudan has a series of royal pyramids in Nubia, built about 800 years after the Egyptians stopped building pyramids. They have very steep sides, around 70 degrees. North America has hundreds of earthen mounds, many of them resembling pyramid shapes as well as being astronomically aligned. One huge pyramid-like mound is found at the site of an ancient civilization, Cahokia, in Illinois. It is evident that this dedication to pyramid-building is worldwide, ultimately stemming from Satan's counterfeit at Babel.

Ziggurats, similar to pyramids, are found mostly in the areas of ancient Mesopotamia. Many people believe the Tower of Babel was most likely in the form of a ziggurat. They have a clear link to Babel, apparently built as a connection between heaven and earth as well as the underworld. They are usually built with seven levels, representing the seven heavens and planes of existence. King Nebuchadnezzar is said to have styled the Boraippa Ziggurat after the Tower of Babel itself! Inscriptions found on a foundation stone explain why he built the structure, and another text quotes Nebuchadnezzar, declaring that the tower should reach to the skies, just as it did at Babel. Ziggurats are common all over the Mesopotamian area, the earliest dating from about 3000 B.C., and the latest about the sixth century B.C. They range from relatively simple structures used only as a raised platform for a temple, such as the White Temple of Uruk, to massive and mathematically complex, such as Etemenanki (meaning "the foundation of heaven and earth") of ancient Babylon. Some of the best-preserved ziggurats include Chogha Zanbil, Sialk, and the ziggurat of Ur.

In North America, earthen mounds still remain as evidence of Babel's influence. There are at least 100,000 still in existence, and thousands more believed to have been destroyed by erosion, farming, and development. The mounds are found in great numbers in and around the area of the Mississippi basin and its tributaries, as well as the fertile plains along the Gulf. Used for ceremonies as well as practical purposes, not much is known about the mound builders.

Jaguar Temple in Tikal— Mesoamerican pyramids.

Poverty Point in northeastern Louisiana.

The Native Americans of the area make no claim on them though they sometimes made use of the structures. It is believed they belonged to an ancient culture that flourished around A.D. 800–1500. Cahokia, located in Illinois, is the site of over 120 mounds. Various artifacts found there have convinced archeologists that it was once a huge, dynamic city with a population of 20,000. The people of this culture were prolific builders, constructing everything from wood and thatch buildings to sun calendars to the monumental earthen mounds that still exist today. These huge mounds were often built in stages, requiring a tremendous amount of time, energy, and soil.[2]

Cahokia boasts the largest man-made mound in North America: Monks Mound. At approximately 100 feet high, it is the dominating feature at Cahokia and one of the only mounds in eastern North America with more than two terraces. Evidence found around the site indicates an advanced society where dance, music, and sport were an important part of daily and ceremonial life. Mound 72 also contains the skeletons of some 300 people, testifying that the brutal practice of human sacrifice was also part of the culture. Another fascinating site of ancient civilization in North America is Poverty Point in northeastern Louisiana. Located on a 25-foot bluff overlooking the Mississippi River floodplain, its overall size and complexity astounds archeologists. The most prominent feature of the site is the six concentric curving earthworks, each one four to six feet high and 140–200 feet apart.

There are other mounds around the site with the "Bird Mound" being the largest. Standing over 70 feet high, it is second only to Monks Mound. Evidence found on other mounds in the area indicates human sacrifice, just as at Cahokia. These two areas contain some of the most preserved mounds ever found and are open to the public to tour. It is surely eye opening to behold these fantastic structures — evidence of intelligent ancient man, right here in North America.

The earthen mounds come in many shapes and sizes. One very popular type of mound, the serpent mound, has eerie connections to the Quetzalcoatl (a god often pictured as a feathered snake) cult of Mexico. Most of them are depicted with the snake eating an egg or with eggs in the general vicinity, bringing to mind Genesis 3:15: "And I will put enmity between you [the serpent] and the woman, and between your seed and her seed." The Great Serpent mound, located in Adams County, Ohio, is a three-foot high, 1,330-foot-long effigy mound in the form of a serpent swallowing an egg. Dated roughly around A.D. 1070, it is the largest serpent mound in the world.

The Great Serpent mound has fascinating astronomical importance. The head aligns with the summer solstice sunset and each coil points to a different heavenly event. Some archeologists believe the mound also aligns with the constellation Draco and others suggest it was inspired by the legends of Uktena, a feathered serpent (much like Quetzalcoatl) with otherworldly powers. Almost a twin to this serpent mound, one has been identi-

2   Claudia Gellman Mink, Cahokia (Cahokia, IL: Cahokia Mounds Society, 1992).

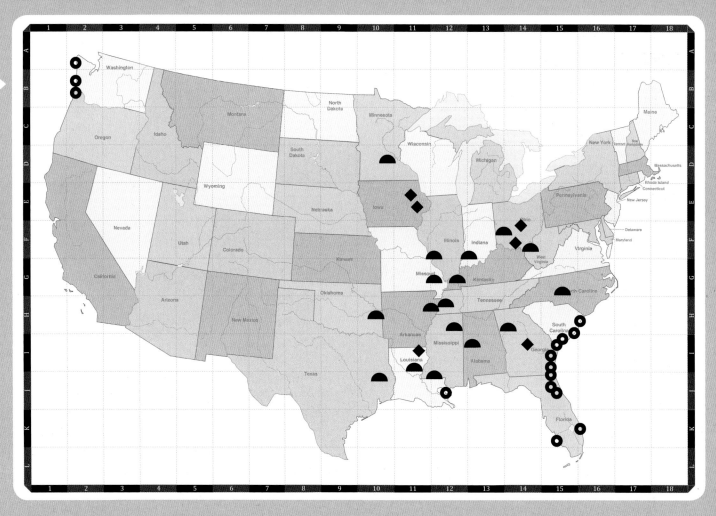

This map highlights a very small sampling of different types of Indian mound sites in the United States. An estimated 100,000 such sites are located across all 48 contiguous states. Mounds have been destroyed or damaged when the dirt forming them was used for construction or agricultural purposes. Many others remain undocumented or excavated. Three types of Indian mounds are found in the United States:

◗ Mounds

F12	Monk's Mound Cahokia (Illinois)
H12	Pinson Mounds (Tennessee)
I13	Moundville Archaeological Park (Alabama)
F14	Fort Ancient (Ohio)
D10	Indian Mounds Regional Park (Minnesota)
F14	Criel Mound (West Virginia)
H12	Nodena Mound site (Arkansas)
I10	Caddo Mounds (Texas)
H10	Spiro Mounds (Oklahoma)
H14	Etowah Indian Mounds (Georgia)
G15	Town Creek Indian Mound (North Carolina)
F13	Angel Mounds (Indiana)
I11	Crooks Mound (Louisiana)
G12	Wycliffe Mounds (Kentucky)
H12	Pharr Mounds (Mississippi)1
I12	Emerald Mound (Mississippi)2

◆ Effigy Mounds: normally in the form of an animal, person or symbol

I11	Bird Mound at Poverty point (Louisiana)
F14	The Great Serpent mound (Ohio)2
E11	Effigy Mounds National Monument (Iowa)
F14	Alligator Effigy Mound (Ohio)1
E11	Marching Bear Mound Group (Iowa)
I14	Rock Hawk Effigy Mound (Georgia)

◉ Shell Mounds: also called middens

These are mounds formed from shells, animal bones, and other items. Found along coastal areas around the world, these areas include South Carolina, Georgia, Florida, Washington, Mississippi, and California.

The Marching Bear Mound Group is an elaborate effigy mound found in Iowa.

fied near Peterborough, Ontario, surrounded by eight smaller oval mounds, which could symbolize eggs. Other serpent mounds, less defined, include mounds found in Alabama, California, Florida, Georgia, Illinois, and Iowa. Even in Scotland there are accounts of serpent mounds near North Ayrshire, said to be sites of serpent and sun worship.

Henges are also found around the world. These astronomically significant circles of stone or wood are found in various sizes and states of disrepair. The most famous is, of course, Stonehenge located in Wiltshire County, England. It was aligned to the summer and winter solstices as well as the most southerly rising and northerly setting of the moon. The ground plan and structural engineering is mathematically sophisticated, though its construction is thought to predate the eastern Mediterranean, Egyptian, and Greek cultures. Originally, it had 60 bluestones, each weighing four tons and coming from Wales, 240 miles away! The largest of the Sarsen stones in the inner ring is estimated at 40 tons and came from 18 miles away. It is still a mystery how the builders were able to move the stones and construct the circle.

There are over 900 stone rings in the British Isles alone, but they are found many other places as well. Perhaps the oldest known stone circle is found in Nabta, Egypt, situated directly on the Tropic of Cancer. In Israel's Golan Heights, the Gilgal Refaim is a huge stone circle consisting of five concentric circles, with its many stones

weighing a total of 37,000 tons. It was an astronomical observatory and stellar calendar.

A stonehenge located in Sweden dates from A.D. 600 and is in the shape of a ship, also aligned with the summer and winter solstices. An Armenian stone circle possibly mirrors the constellation Cygnus, and in the Nubian Desert another marks the summer solstice. Even in the Amazon, located near Sao Paulo, Brazil, the remains of an astronomically aligned stone ring have been found. Americans may be surprised to learn that a "woodhenge" once existed at the site of the ancient civilization at Cahokia in Illinois. As per usual, it marked the solstices and equinoxes. These ancient stone (and wood) rings are undeniably related to astronomy/astrology and therefore have their connection to the religion of Babel. It is evident from their appearance around the world that the different tribes got the technology for creating them and the mathematical skills for aligning them from the same place.

Obelisks, found in various places around the world, are another type of megalithic monument from ancient times. Tall, narrow, four-sided pillars topped with a small pyramid, they were originally carved from a single section of rock. (Modern obelisks, such as the Washington Monument, were built in pieces.) The term "obelisk" comes from the Greek, meaning "nail or "pointed pillar," but most of the ancient, traditional obelisks were erected in Egypt. To the Egyptians, the monuments represented the rays of their sun-god and were typically put up in pairs at the entryways of their temples. According

The fallen obelisk of Hatshepsut at Karnak, Egypt.

Seamless Inca Wall in Cuzco, Peru.

to John Anthony West, an independent Egyptologist, the obelisks were specifically aligned, the angles of the shaft pertaining to the exact longitude and latitude of the specific location. Also, the pair was uneven, one monument being taller than the other, so as to cast a specific shadow which astronomers used as a sort of calendar and observatory.[3] Twenty-nine of these ancient Egyptian obelisks still survive today, residing in different countries around the world, including France, Israel, and Italy. Yet obelisks were not only erected in Egypt. The Assyrians were known to raise obelisk-type monuments to celebrate the achievements of the king. Three have been preserved in the British Museum. There were even obelisk-type stele pillars in the ancient kingdom of Ethiopia.[4] Not considered true obelisks because they do not have four sides or a pyramidal top, they were significantly monolithic structures used as burial markers. In Peru, a monolithic stele monument dates back to Pre-Colombian days. Thought to have originally been located in a Temple Plaza in Chavin, it is covered in iconography and aligned with the equinox sunrise.[5] The exact purpose and/or symbolism behind the obelisks is unknown. Indeed, the multiple conspiracy theories and myths regarding the monuments make it difficult to discern their true significance.

As mentioned in chapter 6, places like Puma Punku with its huge stones and intricate puzzle-like construction also have scientists perplexed. The site, part of the Tiwanaku complex in Bolivia, has many unsolved mysteries. Legend has it that it was built by a race of giants in a single night after the Flood. Indeed, the enormity of the stones suggests giant-like builders and the amazing precision of the stonework seems almost magically engineered. Huge stone slabs, the largest being 120 tons, are thought to be quarried downhill six miles away. Smaller slabs of andesite were quarried 56 miles away across Lake Titicaca! Many of these huge stones were cut with many sides, at angles that fit each other perfectly, making an interlocking system that could withstand the earthquakes in the area. The blocks also show highly developed geometric patterns indicating technology much more advanced than later civilizations in the region. The sophisticated workmanship also includes elaborate drainage systems and well-engineered irrigation canals as well as agricultural terraces. The people of Puma Punku were extremely clever and held many secrets that may never be discovered today. The remnants testifying to their skill are a confirmation of God's amazing work in creating intelligent man.

Huge intricate stone-works, similar to Puma Punku and equally mysterious, can be found in other places as well. Located in Peru, Cuzco, the first Incan capital, bears many similar characteristics to Bolivia's Puma Punku. Built in the shape of a Puma, Cuzco has precisely built walls with stones of various odd angles all fitted so perfectly that a knife blade doesn't fit between them. Near Cuzco, Sacsayhuaman also contains these magnificent structures with stones weighing between 100 and 300 tons! This style of stonework is seen all over Central America and also in the Pacific. Easter Island, for example, and Tahiti both display this fascinating and unexplainable architecture. Somehow all these people

3   TimothyYoungblood, Obelisks of the World, http://www.masters-table.org/pagan/oblis.htm, accessed November 18, 2011.
4   Obelisks, http://www.crystalinks.com/obelisks.html, accessed November 18, 2011.
5   James Jacobs, The Tello Obelisk, a Chavín de Huantár Sculpture, http://www.jqjacobs.net/andes/tello.html, accessed November 18, 2011.

had the same knowledge — this advanced technology that even scientists today cannot figure out.

Even larger stones are found in Lebanon at a city called Baalbek, considered by some archeologists to be a true wonder of the ancient world. The ruins are composed of a massive platform built with more stone than the Great Pyramid of Giza and include three different temples. It is here that three of the largest stones ever cut and moved are found. Named the "Trilithon," they are made of limestone and each weighs 800 tons. Two even larger ones are found nearby, still attached to the bedrock but weighing around 1,000 tons each! The stones in the Trilithon are laid end to end on top of a six-layer retaining wall. The fifth layer contains at least 24 stones that weigh 300 tons each! Ingeniously built, the lower layers are made of smaller stones (though still very large) allowing for the bottom layers to move with the earth during earthquakes. The origin of the complex is unknown, with various legends claiming the builder was Cain, Nimrod, Solomon, or even a race of giants.

Interestingly, there are structures with these same characteristics: unexplainable, extremely advanced, and megalithic, under water along many coastlines. Researcher Dr. Masaaki Kimura, as well as Graham Hancock, believes ancient men built these cities and monuments during the Ice Age before the water levels were so high. Indeed, the ocean shoreline could have been as much as 150 feet lower than it is today due to all the ice. It would make sense that the Ice Age civilizations would have built along the coast, just as people do today, and when the water levels rose, their ancient cities were flooded and hidden, waiting to be found. Off the coast of Japan there is an underwater monument called Yanagi. Though there is some debate about whether this is a man-made structure or not, evidence seems to suggest it was not formed through natural oceanic processes.

Dwarka, off the coast of India, is actually known in ancient Indian literature. The ruins of the city include many anchors, which lead archeologists to believe Dwarka was a busy port city in its time. In the Yucatan Channel near Cuba there exists evidence of an extensive urban civilization with megalithic construction. Archeologists surmise it may predate all known American cultures.

Off the coast of Lebanon, the ancient city of Yarmuta may have been found after being concealed for 3,000 years. Diver El-Sarji has photographed a broad central square, streets, temples, and statues of Egyptian gods at the site.[6] In the summer of 2011, Pavlopetri, off the coast of Greece, became the first underwater city to be fully digitally mapped and recorded. Archeologists have since discovered that this ancient city was much like our port cities today; not a village of farmers but a stratified, well-designed society where people had professions. There are many more of these underwater cities that give evidence to the Ice Age as well as the intelligent ancient men who lived at that time. Unfortunately, few of the sites have been sufficiently explored and excavated, so there is little concrete information available.

Examples such as the ones described above give clear evidence that very little is really known about ancient man's intelligence level. It is obvious that the ancient architects held some sort of knowledge that is unknown today. It's interesting that cultures able to build such magnificent structures are often not even credited with having a system of writing or any scientific knowledge. Yet, starting with solid biblical presuppositions, these fascinating buildings only support the creation story of Genesis as well as the dispersion at Babel. Since God created man intelligent and with very long life spans, His story is only confirmed by the sophistication evident in ancient architecture. Since man worked collectively at Babel to build a city and a tower, it makes sense that similar styles of building, fashioned after those first structures, would be found in the cultures that spread out from Babel. So you see, the data and the physical hard evidence does not contradict the Bible but rather confirms the record of Scripture.

6   Dan Vergano, "Sunken Cities Surface in Time," http://www.usatoday.com/news/world/june01/2001-06-28-sunken-cities.htm, accessed October 10, 2011.

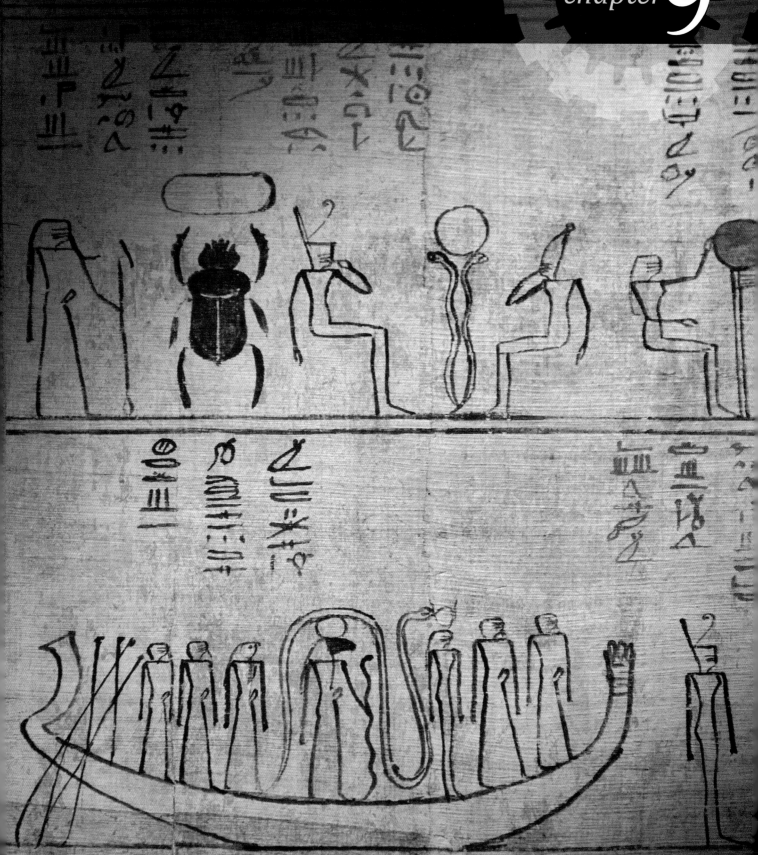

chapter 9

Religions and Legends

It is not surprising, working from a biblical perspective, that a study of religions will reveal that many cultures were monotheistic at their early stages. This reflects the early knowledge of the Creator God. Bill Cooper, in his book *After the Flood*, states that even pagan man "was indeed aware of God and of His attributes and power, and that this awareness had existed and flourished for centuries without any recourse at all to the scriptures." This quote only confirms what the Bible states in Romans 1:20: "For since the creation of the world His invisible attributes, His eternal power and divine nature, have been clearly seen, being understood through what has been made, so that they [mankind] are without excuse." Cooper quotes Thales of Miletus (ca 625–545 B.C.), credited as the first materialist philosopher among the Greeks: "Of existing things, God is the oldest — for he is ungenerated. The world is the most beautiful, for it is God's creation." When historians try to assert that Judeo-Christian beliefs are relatively recent in history, they are ignoring the facts. People knew about God, the one Creator God, even in ancient times. Interestingly, Cooper goes on to describe how Plato recognized that the ideas of naturalism would "ruin the younger generation, both in the state at large and in private families."[1] Mankind is built religious; he does not benefit from rejecting God.

Evidence of the worldwide knowledge of the Creator God ranges from the Ican god Viracocha to the ancient Chinese god Shang Ti, both of which bear striking similarity to the Jewish Yahweh. The Karen people of Burma also have a god, Y'wa, who "is eternal, his life is long . . . He is perfect in meritorious attributes. . . . Y'wa created the world in the beginning!"[2] As is discussed later in the chapter, cultures around the world have creation myths that are unbelievably similar to the original truth of Genesis.

In his book *Eternity in their Hearts*, Don Richardson sites the testimonies of missionaries who have witnessed to various people groups and found remnants of Judeo-Christian beliefs in their religions. This confirms the account in Acts 14:16–17 that says God "permitted all the nations to go their own ways; and yet He did not leave Himself without witness. . . ." Richardson relates the study of Dr. Wilhelm Schmidt, an Austrian who, in the early 20th century, attempted to compile every example of "native monotheism" from around the world. When Schmidt had finished his research in 1955 "he had accumulated more than 4,000 pages of evidence in a total of 12 large volumes!" Richardson found other customs similar among many religions such as a city of refuge, a scapegoat, a peace agreement with a "rebirth" ritual, and a peace agreement involving the giving of the chief's son to the other tribe.[3]

It is evident that all these parallel religions had to come from some ultimate original. Of course, at first, everyone knew the truth. Noah would have shared the original account of creation, the Fall, and the precepts of God with his children and grandchildren. As these beliefs were passed down through the generations they would slowly be perverted. The vague distortions that exist today contain very little truth and it is clear to see how Satan has continued to pervert God's message to the nations.

Commonalities in religion are not limited to ancient monotheistic beliefs, however. In the very earliest religions there are common deity characters. Interestingly, the three most popular beings appear to be based off of the biblical persons of Nimrod, Cush, and Semiramis. Though their names differ around the world with the different languages, their stories and characteristics reveal them to be the same.

Various names for:			
Nimrod ▶	Osiris	Bacchus	Baal
Cush ▶	Hermes	Ra	Valcan
Semiramis ▶	Isis	Vishnu	Madonna

---

1   Bill Cooper, *After the Flood* (West Sussex, England: New Wine Press, 1995), p. 15–23.
2   "The Concept of Monotheism in Ancient Times," http://www.submission.info/perspectives/monotheism/monotheism_since_ancient_times.html, accessed September 15, 2011.
3   Don Richardson, *Eternity in Their Hearts* (Regel Books 1981), Chapter 4, page 141; Ernest Brandewie, *Wilhelm Schmidt and the Origin of the Idea of God* (Lanham, MD: Rowman and Littlefield, 1983).

Alexander Hyslop, a researcher from the middle 1800s, traced the commonness of these religions around the world in symbols, deities, and practices. In his book *The Two Babylons,* he makes the argument, declaring that each of the major religions around the world is simply a slightly distorted rendering of the perversion created at Babel.[4]

Another religious mystery surrounds the zodiac and the "heavenly bodies." The same star maps and constellations can be found in almost every culture that studies the heavens. This seems to confirm the supposition that these religions probably all come from Babel, which, due to its goal of reaching to the heavens, likely had a strong focus on the stars. Not only do many of the constellations symbolize various deities, the ancient people aligned many of their monuments and temples to different star signs. Along with star signs, there are hundreds of buildings that are perfectly aligned to the summer and winter solstices and equinoxes. For some reason, these ancient people were fascinated with the heavens. Many cultures also have similar worship of the sun, moon, stars, and planets. Evidently they found great meaning in the signs of the night sky that may never be fully understood by today's scholars.

Along with the common religions come the myths and legends. To avoid confusion, the word "myth" in this section is defined as "a story that may or may not be true." William Bascom explains that myths and legends are generally regarded as fact, though myths describe more distant events than legends.[5] A surprising number of cultures around the world have similar legends about creation, the Flood, Babel, and the Ice Age.

CREATION LEGENDS

Generally speaking, there are two main myths about the origin of the earth: some god(s) created everything or everything developed without any external help. This section will focus on similar creation legends that show that throughout the world, mankind had knowledge about how things began. As the nations spread out from Babel, they took the stories and teachings of Noah and his sons and just like religions were distorted over time, so were the original myths and legends.

When asked about the religious beliefs of ancient races, author and researcher Jonathan Gray answered: "According to the evidence, at first they all generally believed in one Creator who had made mankind. They also believed they had rebelled against him and were guilty of breaking his laws."[1] Researcher Stephen Langdon, of Oxford University, had a similar view, which he publicized in 1931, explaining that the older civilizations were monotheistic and that they declined over the years into a state of polytheism.[2] Still further, Bill Cooper, author of *After the Flood,* declares that all the major ancient cultures held a belief that a supreme divine being created the universe.[3]

All over the world the ancient legends confirm these statements. In the Egyptian "Book of the Dead"[4] there is a hymn to the god Amen-Ra in which it is said, "O Maker of the Gods, who hast stretched out the heavens and founded the earth! . . . He maketh the green herb whereon the cattle live, and the staff of life whereon mean live. He maketh the Fish to live in the rivers, and the feathered fowl in the sky. . . . Hail to thee, O thou maker of all these things, thou ONLY ONE."[5] Ancient texts from Heliopolis, Egypt, state clearly: "I am the creator of all things that exist . . . that came forth from my mouth"[6] Evidently the ancient peoples of Egypt were not ignorant to the Creator God and

4 Alexander Hyslop, *The Two Babylons* (Ontario, CA: Chick Publications, 1998).
5 Charles Martin, *Flood Legends* (Green Forest, AR: Master Books, 2009).

1 Jonathan Gray, "Questions and Answers," accessed April 27, 2011, http://beforeus.com/questions_answers.html.
2 Adnan Oktar, "Distortion of the True Religion," accessed November 10, 2011, http://www.thestoneage.org/stone_age_03_a.php.
3 Cooper, *After the Flood,* p. 18.
4 The Egyptian "Book of the Dead" was a collection of magic spells, hymns, and formulas designed to be a sort of guidebook to the afterlife. They began to appear in Egyptian tomes around 1600 b.c.
5 "The Concept of Monotheism Since Ancient Times," accessed August 30, 2011, http://www.submission.info/perspectives/monotheism/monotheism_since_ancient_times.html.
6 Cooper, *After the Flood,* p. 17.

His supremacy. Other aspects of the same hymn portray Amen-Ra as the creator of light, kind-hearted to the oppressed, uttering wisdom, and speaking words of truth. The clear connection to the Almighty God of Israel is hard to ignore. Indeed, Bill Cooper asserts that never in Egypt's long history is there any record of anyone coming against the common belief of creation by divine forces.

It is not only Egypt in which this distinct similarity occurs. In Grecian legends, "out of Chaos came Mother Earth." The ancient Greeks believed that "Father Sky" made rain fall upon the earth and gave her sunshine to produce plants, birds, and animals. Furthermore, their story of Pandora opening a box of evil gifts and loosing them on the world is eerily similar to the biblical story of Eve and the Fall of man. The Phoenicians begin their creation legends with, "In the beginning all was dark and windy."[7] In the Gayatri Mantra, the Hindi people meditate on "God, his glorious attributes, who is the basis of everything in this universe as its Creator, who is fit to be worshiped as Omnipresent, Omnipotent, Omniscient, and self-existent conscious being."[8] Again, there is that distinct similarity to the God of the Bible. Finally, legends from Cambodia portray knowledge of the original perfect creation: "In the time of that most excellent of Yugas (ages) everything had been done and nothing remained to be done . . . there was no disease or decline of the organs of sense through the influence of age . . . no malice . . . no hatred, cruelty, fear, affliction, jealousy, or envy. . . ."[9] This is just a sampling of the hundreds of creations legends found worldwide. Yet even with these few, it is clear that the ancient nations had to have some sort of connection and that their myths and legends come from a common source.

FLOOD LEGENDS

Just as with creation legends, ancient Flood legends abound. Dr. A.J. Monty White and Dr. Duane Gish claim that there are more than 270 flood legends from cultures worldwide, while Graham Hancock claims there are more than 500.[1] In his book *Flood Legends,* Charles Martin compares and contrasts many different accounts of the Flood, focusing on the Genesis account, the story out of the Mahabharata from India, and a legend coming from the Karina people of Venezuela. Similarities between these legends and hundreds of others range from crew members on the boat to the use of animals in the story.

In the different legends, there are different aspects that remain true to the original biblical story as well as interesting distortions. The Mahabharata, the Karina legend, and the Bible all declare that only eight people were rescued on the ark. In some other legends there are as few as two people, but it is interesting to note that with the decline of people, the magic used in the re-creation of the world increases (legends from Burma, New Guinea, and Greece for example). The Karina legend is also remarkably similar to the biblical account in that two of every animal and a seed from every plant is taken on board the boat. The legend from the Hareskin tribe of North America describes an old man on a raft collecting drowning animals two-by-two. In many of the legends, animals are used in some way as a sort of "litmus test" to discern if the land is dry. Noah sends out a raven and two doves (or one dove twice) while in the *Epic of Gilgamesh* from Babylon, a dove, swallow, and raven are sent out. The Hareskin Indians say that a muskrat and then a beaver are sent to touch the bottom and then a fox is sent out to run on the dry land. In Timor, the legend says that animals were thrown into the Flood to appease the god in order that he might withdraw the waters. A rooster crows to indicate dry land in the myth from China.

One fascinating detail to note is the global impact of the Flood in most these legends. Usually, if the myth is clearly defined as being local, it is referring to a smaller flood in that tribe's history, not the ancient

7   Ruth Beechick, *Genesis, Finding our Roots* (Pollock Pines, CA: Arrow Press, 1997), p. 19, 39.
8   "The Concept of Monotheism Since Ancient Times," accessed August 30, 2011, http://www.submission.info/perspectives/monotheism/monotheism_since_ancient_times.html.
9   Hancock, *Heaven's Mirror*, p. 154.

1   A.J. Monty White, "Flood Legends: The Significance of a World of Stories Based on Truth," March 29, 2007, accessed April 25, 2011, http://www.answeringenesis.org/articles/am/v2/n2/flood-legends; Hancock, *Fingerprints of the Gods*, p. 193.

one of Noah. The Mahabharata clearly states, "all was sea" and "all ends in violent water." In the Icelandic epic, the "mountains dash together . . . and heaven is split in two . . . and the earth sinks into the sea." A legend from New Zealand declares that the earth was completely changed and not one soul was left alive. In the Greek legend, Zeus parted the mountains, enabling the flood to spread and cover the entire earth. The Montagnais peoples of North America say that no land could be seen on any side, and the *Epic of Gilgamesh* states, "nothing could be seen but cloudy, murky water." Almost every major culture, even the highly advanced ones, have global deluge stories indicating an event bigger than a mere local flood.

Many people try to say that the writers of the Bible were influenced by these hundreds of other legends, most notably the *Epic of Gilgamesh* but, as outlined in chapter 2, God has priority when He writes something, for He is outside of time and without error. Moreover, of all of the accounts, the Bible actually has the most reasonable story. From the seaworthy dimensions of the ark, to the amount of time spent in the boat, to the purpose of animals and cargo, the biblical account makes sense! The other stories usually have improbable magic involved or ridiculous boats such as the cube in the *Epic of Gilgamesh* or the canoe of an Australian legend. As cultures change and memory fades, the accounts are altered to suit the tellers. Details change as each culture develops its own sets of beliefs and practices. Changes also occur depending on where the story is told; the different animals used usually coincide with the animals in the area of that legend. Do not allow this multitude of legends to unnerve you! Thank God for the confirmation of His word, for they are all merely perversions of His original story.

Comparisons between the different accounts from the different cultures can be seen in the following chart:

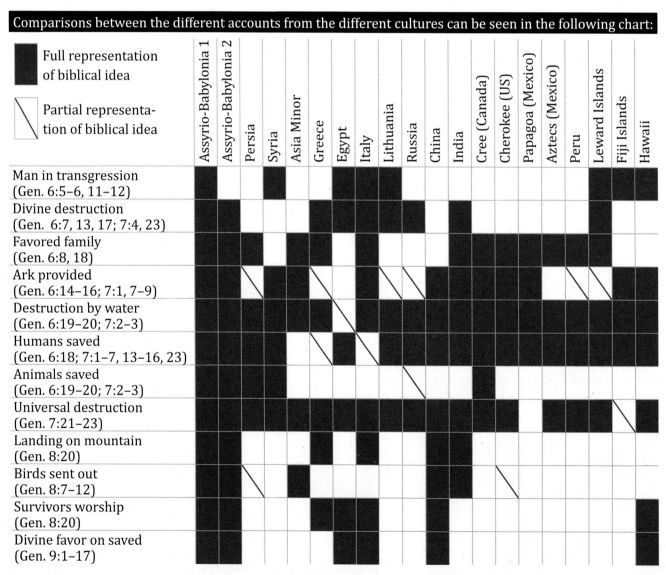

BABEL LEGENDS

Concerning legends about Babel, Charles Martin reveals how people all over the world also have similar stories about building a structure to reach the heavens or their god(s). In Burma, the story is remarkably similar: the people built a pagoda to reach into heaven and their god came down and confused their languages in wrath, dispersing them around the globe. Sometimes the stories will not contain all the biblical concepts regarding the confusion of languages and the tower, but will have one or the other.

In the Congo, the legend says that the people balanced on poles. In the Mexican version, the tower is built of clay. India has a myth in which a group of demons attempted to build an altar to the sky but they were thwarted by the sky-god. The Ba-Luyi tribe of Africa tells a legend of a great tower made of masts, built to reach the sun-god, which fell because of instability and killed everyone involved. In Greece, legend has it that Hermes separated the peoples into nations by introducing languages as some sort of divine practical joke. The people of Assam believe a band of warriors was attacking a python when suddenly they found themselves unable to understand each other and were forced to separate into new tribes. Each myth in itself is not necessarily true, nor does it prove the truth of the biblical account. However, the universality of the legends and the fact that many are so similar gives credibility that the event actually happened.

Many believe that the Sumerian Etemenanki ziggurat of Babylon, which was built by Nabopolassar and Nebuchadnezzar in the sixth century B.C., is a reconstruction of the Tower of Babel. Nebuchadnezzar wrote that a former king had built a tower, "but he did not complete its head. Since a remote time, people had abandoned it, without order expressing their words." He explains how it has been eroded and destroyed since then.[1] Ancient historian Herodotus describes this ziggurat as well. This could very well be a reconstruction of the Tower of Babel, for indeed, there are many such reconstructions in different shapes and sizes found all over the world due to the dispersion of the peoples and their new religion.

1   Mario Seiglie, "Answers from Genesis — Part 7," accessed April 30, 2011, http://www.verticalthought.org/issues/vt26/answers-genesis.htm.

ICE AGE LEGENDS

Legends about the Ice Age should be common because the ancient people would have experienced the situation first hand. Graham Hancock gives many examples of people groups that have legends of "the Great Cold" or "evil winters." Such people groups include those of the Zoroastrian religion, the Toba Indians in South America, the Mayans as described in the Mayan Popol Vuh, the Incas, the Tarahumara of northern Mexico, the Araucanians of Chile, the Mataco Indians of Argentina, and many more. Hancock explains how many of these cultures associate the Flood to a subsequent period of cold, volcanism, earthquakes, mountain shaping, and periods of darkness and endless clouds — thus the sun was unable to warm the earth's surface. He gives numerous examples that show that there must have been a lot of volcanism and a quick deep freeze in some places. Hancock states that "the Mayan Popol Vuh associates the flood, with 'much hail, black rain and mist, and indescribable cold' " and he continues that other Mayan sources say "sunlight did not return till the twenty-sixth year after the flood."[1] This is all very consistent to what we would expect from a biblical view of an ice age.

1   Hancock, Fingerprints of the Gods, p. 207–223.

chapter 10

" *His brother's name was Jubal; he was the father of all those who play the lyre and pipe.*"

—*Genesis 4:21*

MUSIC AND ART

Music is something common to people all over the world, although it has distinctive styles depending on where you go. Why is music so important to mankind? It is used in ceremonies, religious practices, recreation, battles, etc. But where did it begin and why is it so universal? From Genesis 4, it is evident that music and instruments have been around since before the flood. Jubal was "the father of all those who play the lyre and pipe" (4:21). Since that time, music has been prevalent in most cultures. Music, with rhythm and time, demonstrates a sophisticated culture, advanced enough to spend time in the arts rather than simply farming and hunting at all times. The Bible is filled with many examples of musical instruments and of songs and psalms composed by men of those times. And it is not only the Bible that gives us evidence of music.

In Greek mythology, the "pan-pipe" was the invention of the god Pan and has been known since 2500 B.C. It was known as the instrument of shepherds and was tuned by putting wax into the tube to achieve the right tune. The aulos has also been known since ancient times. In classical Greece it was common for two to be played at once until Roman times when playing the single aulos became the norm. Stringed instruments also have a long history dating from 2000 B.C. in Mesopotamia. Percussion instruments have also been common. Rattles, drums, and tambourines have been found and pictured in ancient drawings and carvings. Even the first organ was invented in the second century B.C.! Something as technical as the organ would require a great amount of intelligence and time to perfect.[1]

One interesting thing is that the King's Chamber in the Great Pyramid is tuned to the F sharp chord. F sharp is supposedly the fundamental frequency that is produced by the earth. Researcher Boris Said claims "the Indian Shamans tuned their ceremonial flutes to F sharp because it is a frequency that is sacred to 'Mother Earth.' "[2]

Also, remarkably similar instruments are used in cultures all around the world. The aulos pipe has been found in Greece, Java, Bolivia, Peru, and even the bagpipes of Scotland and Ireland are forms of aulos. The bullroarer instrument has been used in Australia, Egypt, the British Isles, Scotland, and New Guinea, and by the Inuit of Northern Canada, the Dogon in Africa, the Maori, and almost all of the tribes of North American Indians. It has been used in many different religious festivals, and even to help heal people by vibration similar to modern ultrasound or massage therapy. Flutes are also very common among cultures and appear to be one of the oldest instruments. Professor Chris Stringer says that the flutes found in Europe "provide yet more evidence of the sophistication of the people that lived at that time."[3] Other professors confirm this idea, also noting that humanity's creative spirit was much more developed in ancient times than usually granted them.

Youth playing the aulos, detail of a banquet scene. Tondo of an Attic red-figure cup, ca. 460 BC–450 BC.

1   Kristof De Jaeger, "Ancient Music Instruments," accessed November 10, 2011, http://realize.be/ancient/framese.html.

2   Childress, *Technology of the Gods,* p. 85–86.
3   Professor Chris Stringer, Natural History Museum, BBC News, June 25, 2009.

The Hagia Triada Mycenaean sarcophagus, 14th century B.C., depicting the earliest lyre with seven strings, held by a man with long robe, third from the left.

Musicians playing the salpinx (trumpet) and the hydraulis (water organ). Terracotta figurine made in Alexandria, first century B.C. From Alexandria.

Bronselurer found in Brudevælte, Denmark, discovered in 1797.

Imagine playing drums on a shark! The top of this drum from Hawaii is made of shark skin tied with coconut string. The drum is called a pahu hula - it made music to go with dancing and poetry. Drum (pahu hula) from Hawaii, pre-18th century A.D.

Isis holding a sistrum and an oinochoe. Marble, Roman artwork from the Adrian period (117–138 A.D.).

ART

Art from ancient times also testifies to this creative spirit. Cave art, pictures on pottery, and carvings on walls depict ancient legends, practices, and religious ideas throughout history. There are many examples that portray advanced artistry techniques even in ancient times. In France, the Chauvet caves display artwork that is supposedly 32,000 years old (according to the old-earth paradigm), yet archeologists consider it more sophisticated than much younger examples. A 3,000-year-old stone lion was found in southeastern Turkey, causing researchers to re-evaluate the cultural advancement of the Neo-Hitttite Kingdom of Patina.[4] Mayan art, including pottery and sculptures, has often been praised as some of the most sophisticated of its time. Unlike most cultures, the Mayans were particularly adept at realistically portraying humans and dedicated to details. China has also been heralded for its spectacular and unusual ancient art forms.

Painting from the Chauvet cave, replica in the Brno museum Anthropos.

Stone lion sculpture that adorned the Tayinat citadel gate.

So a study of ancient music and art proves that ancient cultures were not made up of brutish animals. The people cared about beauty, art, and music. This appreciation of beauty is unique to mankind. It is part of our created humanity, something that could not come from a slow evolution from animals.

4   Jennifer Welsh, "Stone Lion Reveals Sophisticated Ancient Culture," Live Science, http://www.livescience.com/15486-3000-year-lion-statue-gate.html, accessed September 23, 2011.

chapter 11

"Declaring the end from the beginning,
And from ancient times things which have not been done,
Saying, 'My purpose will be established,
And I will accomplish all My good pleasure'"

—Isaiah 46:10

Babel is not Gone

One of the principles of apologetics is to project a view to its final conclusion. This is how you *apply* presuppositional thinking. We began this book with a bias: God exists and He created the world.

We laid out 3 arguments:

- God has priority in sequence and time and His Word is true and His analysis of man is correct.
- Since God created man, ancient humans were very intelligent from the beginning.
- The Tower of Babel was a real event in which mankind collectively rebelled against God, forming their own religion, and their dispersion around the world is evident in the commonalities found in ancient cultures everywhere.

Working from these arguments, we have found that the evidence discovered all over the earth confirms the historical record of the Bible and our ultimate starting point: God's existence. We have discovered that ancient man, from the *beginning,* was intelligent.

Through this study we hope that you have come out with more than just facts about ancient civilizations. Our goal is to provide you with apologetic material that not only gives you confidence in the Word of God but also encourages and strengthens you in your outreach. God's sovereignty is clearly revealed throughout history. His plans and purposes, His original truths, are warped and woofed throughout even the most pagan practices (though they may be perverted almost beyond recognition). He has not left Himself without a witness on this earth, and even though Satan has tried to distort His truth, even the counterfeit cannot completely hide the core concepts of God. We hope that this book has taught you how to look at the world around you, to see the counterfeit, to recognize the lies, and to defend the truth. We pray that this book has helped to rewrite history in your mind and heart and has given you a few more "pieces of the puzzle" to fit into place. We pray that it has

firmly founded in you the principle that the Word of God should be *your* starting point in everything.

Along with all of that, there is another thing we would like to share with you. Our study confirms a very important concept that we cannot ignore and do not wish to avoid. The Bible makes various predictions about the future end of the world and, ironically, our study of ancient times gives us great insight into that future end. It is clear that the serpent from the Garden has plans for the future. His passion to be like God, his fight against God's authority, will continue until the end of time. The world empire that Satan began at Babel will rise again in a final attempt to reach his goal.

That's right — Babel is not gone. Of course, as this book has illustrated, the concepts of Babel were never destroyed but spread out over the entire earth and have become entrenched in cultures everywhere, disguised as a counterfeit to God's design.

We hope you have enjoyed our book and been challenged by it. Our final warning and encouragement to you is that you would not only study and understand the past, watch for the counterfeit and defend the truth in the present, but also that you prepare for the future. Be on guard. Be alert. Be ready.

Circa 540 B.C, The wrath of God over Belshazzar's feast signifies impending doom for Babylon.

chapter 12

MORE PIECES OF THE ANCIENT MAN PUZZLE

Through this book we have sought to provide evidence that confirms the truth of God's Word and confirmation to your Christian faith. However, because of the nature of the subject and the connections that can be made to the occult, we want to again warn you as you study for yourself. Be careful; be a Berean (Acts 17:10–11), and take everything back to the Bible. For just as Paul says in 2 Corinthians 10:5, we want to encourage you to destroy "speculations and every lofty thing raised up against the knowledge of God" and be careful to take "every thought captive to the obedience of Christ." Some of the data presented includes ancient legends, religions, and cultural practices that we are not promoting, only using to display further evidence that supports our presuppositions. We would like to warn you as you search deeper into such things, for though they can be used to confirm biblical accounts; such things are not necessarily of God.

DRAGONS

Dragons have seemed to play an important role in the history of the world. There are legends from around the globe describing terrifying creatures unlike any we see today. They are displayed on flags and shields, armor and buildings — their existence undeniable to some. Yet even with all their history and popularity they are considered mythical. The Oxford Dictionary defines a dinosaur as a mythical monster like a giant reptile. In European tradition, the dragon is typically fire-breathing and tends to symbolize chaos or evil, whereas in East Asia it is usually a beneficent symbol of fertility associated with water and the heavens.

But are they mythical? Were there once dragon-like animals roaming our planet? Even the Bible describes some animals with characteristics that cannot be ascribed to any creature alive today. Job speaks of two distinctly different creatures that would fall under that category of a dragon

or perhaps a dinosaur. "Behold now, Behemoth, which I made as well as you; he eats grass like an ox. Behold now, his strength in his loins and his power in the muscles of his belly. He bends his tail like a cedar; the sinews of his thighs are knit together. His bones are tubes of bronze; his limbs are like bars of iron" (Job 40:15–18).

In the following chapter, Job then describes another creature that seems to breathe fire and lives in the sea. "His sneezes flash forth light, and his eyes are like the eyelids of the morning. Out of his mouth go burning torches; sparks of fire leap forth. Out of his nostrils smoke goes forth as from a boiling pot and burning rushes" (Job 41:18–20).

These descriptions are most definitely not a hippopotamus or an alligator as some Bible notes indicate. Based upon a literal, authoritative understanding of Scripture, we must understand that these creatures once existed upon the face of the earth, and walked the earth with mankind. Of course, this would contradict the evolutionary time scale and so the option is rejected by mainstream science. Yet according to the Bible, God would have created dinosaurs along with the rest of the animals and so man would indeed have lived among these giants of the past. It is likely that dragon legends and sightings could come from contact with the dinosaurs before they died out.

GIANTS

In regards to giants, legends and depictions abound as well. The Bible itself gives many accounts describing men of great size:

He killed an Egyptian, a man of great stature five cubits tall. Now in the Egyptian's hand was a spear like a weaver's beam, but he went down to him with a club and snatched the spear from the Egyptian's hand and killed him with his own spear (1 Chronicles 11:23).

Then a champion came out from the armies of the Philistines named Goliath, from Gath, whose height was six cubits and a span (1 Samuel 17:4).

(For only Og king of Bashan was left of the remnant of the Rephaim. Behold, his bedstead was an iron bedstead; it is in Rabbah of the sons of Ammon. Its length was nine cubits and its width four cubits by ordinary cubit) (Deuteronomy 3:11).

Other evidence of giants is found in the world around us:

- In the Golan Heights there is a tomb for a giant, suggested to be Og.

- Arab tradition states that the Trilithon stones at Baalbek and its early temples were built by giants.

- There exists a tall African tribe, average males being near 7 feet tall.

- Fossil record shows better atmospheric conditions for larger things and there are fossils of giant insects and other creatures, much larger than they exist today.

CHINESE LANGUAGE

Another fascinating evidence of man's common ancestry and the Tower of Babel is found in the ancient pictographs of the Chinese language. Amazingly, biblical concepts are found hidden within the 40,000 characters that make up one of the rare Chinese dialects. For example, the symbol for "garden" is made up of the picture letters for "dust, breath, two persons, and enclosure." The verb "to desire/covet" is a picture symbolizing two trees and a woman. The word "boat" is made up of the symbols for "vessel, eight, and mouth (signifying persons)." The more one studies this ancient language, the more biblical truths can be discovered. Many of the symbols are undeniably connected to Scripture and biblical teachings.

Garden paradise Gen 2:8

"Enclosure with 4 rivers" Or "perfect garden"

Stars

...and let them be for signs and for seasons."

This verse in Genesis 1:14 implies that God placed the stars in the sky to tell us something. Scientists inform us that there are over 100 billion galaxies

in the universe, averaging 200 billion stars each. God has given each of these stars a name (Psalm 147:4), and since God does not do anything without purpose, it would seem to us these names must have meaning. Further, Job mentions several constellations by name that were made by God (Job 9:9) and whose movements are directed by Him (Isaiah 40:26).

Unfortunately, throughout history, Satan has used God's pure and unadulterated creation for deception and has led men to worship the creature rather than the Creator.

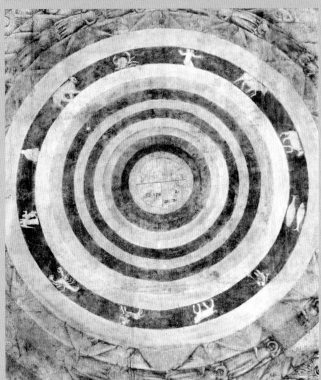

14th century theological cosmography chart.

Flight

Some ancient man researchers, especially David Hatcher Childress, speculate that ancient men had flying techniques. There have been numerous small artifacts found as well as ancient writings and legends pertaining to the ability to fly. If ancient men actually had these capabilities, no physical machinery or craft has ever been found, but representations and descriptions discovered all over the world allow for this possibility, though many of the theories are based on speculations.

▷ In the Mayan areas of Central and South America, small, intricate models (dated around A.D. 500–800) have been found which seem to resemble modern-day airplanes.

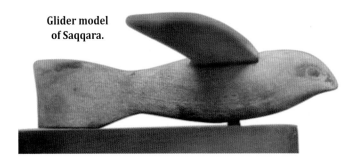

Glider model of Saqqara.

▷ The Saqqara Bird, found in 1898 at a burial site in Egypt, has been tested in computer simulations and with the addition of a tail fin flies quite well.

▷ Hieroglyphs found at the Temple of Osiris in Abydos, Egypt, include strange symbols that look like a modern plane, a helicopter, and even a submarine.

▷ Geoglyphs, massive formations and pictures on the ground best seen from the sky, can be found all over the world and appear to have no real purpose.

▷ From Babylon, there is mention of flight in the law-book called Halkatha that reads "to operate a flying machine is a great privilege. Knowledge of flying is most ancient, a gift of the gods of old for saving lives."

- There are many legends and accounts from China, such as Emperor Shun (2258–2208 B.C.) who "not only constructed a flying apparatus but even made a parachute." Emperor Cheng Tang had a flying chariot made for him by the inventor Ki-Kung-Shi around the time of 1766 B.C. The third century B.C. poet Chu Yun wrote about his adventures in a jade chariot in China and the Gobi Desert.

- The idea of ancient aircraft is not paranormal to Indian people, because their sacred texts (*Samarangana Sutradhara,* the *Ramayana,* writings about the mysterious Rama Empire, and the *Vymaanika Shaastra*) include descriptions of flight.

- Thirteenth century friar Roger Bacon wrote about chariots moving at unimaginable speeds without horses, and seagoing vessels of great velocity.

Whether the above legends and writings have any merit or not, it's well recorded that throughout history many people have tried to fly by the use of wings attached to their arms, and consequently many died jumping from the top of towers and such. Evidently, whether they succeeded or not, ancient man had a great interest in discovering the secrets of flight.

SITES DISPLAYING ANCIENT ADVANCED TECHNOLOGY

We still don't know how they did it. That is perhaps the most intriguing comment when it comes to studying the ancient buildings, cities, and artifacts of ancient man. This evidence defies a description of early man as shown in the evolutionary model by presenting artistry, achievement, creativity, practical aspects of engineering and construction in altering their world, forming organized cities with 'modern' conveniences related to sanitation, and even advanced study and knowledge of the universe.

Kailasa Temple, India

Mayapan, Mexico

Machu Picchu, Peru

Machu Piccu, Peru

Angkor Wat temple, Cambodia

Sphinx, Egypt

Trilithon stone at Baalbek (ancient Heliopolis), Lebanon.

Tikal, Guatemala

Chichen Itza, Mexico

Taj Mahal, India

Petra, Jordan

Yonaguni Monument, Japan

MYSTERIOUS SITES

Sometimes it seems the more we know in terms of science and technology, the less we know because more questions are raised than answered. Such is the case with mysterious sites that are studied extensively, yet the genius of ancient man still manages to elude the understanding or explanations of modern researchers.

Casa Rinconada, New Mexico

Aramu Muru, Lake Titicaca, Peru

Nazca Lines, Peru

Cliff Palace, United States

Coral Castle, Florida

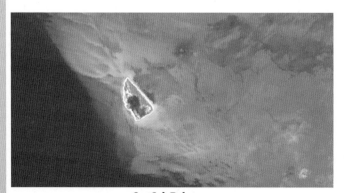

Cay Sal, Bahamas

Stonehenge, England

MONUMENTS AROUND THE WORLD

(Pyramids, Ziggurats, Mounds, Temples, etc.)

These ancient monuments also hint at a compelling similarity to Babel. Many were made as a way to get closer to, or as the home of, gods. Whether serving religious or funerary purposes, these monuments are reminders of the skill and desires of ancient man to interact with gods, become like gods, or find an enternal place beyond death.

Votive Pyramid, Mexico

Cerros, Belize

Lamanai, Belize

Altun-Ha, Belize

Caracol, Belize

Xunantich, Belize

El Castillo, Chichen Itza, Mexico

Niche Pyramid, Mexico

Tomb of the General (Pyramid of the East) , China

Akapana, Bolivia

Tomb of Liu Kuan, Shuangru Mountain, China

Ohio snake mound.

Terracotta Army, Qin Shi Huang's mausoleum, China

Pyramid of Gathering, Tibet, China

Egypt (over 100, especially Giza)

Chalchuapa site, Tazumal, El Salvador

Falicon, France

Great Cairn of Barnenez, France

Pyramid of Hellinkon, Greece

Mirador, Guatemala

Tikal, Guatemala

Candi Sukuh, Java

Hieroglyphic Stairway, Copán, Honduras

Angkor Wat, Cambodia

Prambanan, Indonesia

Xochicalco, Mexico

Huallamarca Pyramid, Peru

Túcume, Peru

Pachacamac Pyramid, Peru

Pyramids of Guima, Canary Islands, Spain

Nubian Pyramids, Sudan

Easter Island, Chile

Marae of Mahaiatea, Tahiti

Mt Nemrut, Turkey

Silbury Hill, England

Choqa Zanbil, Iran

Great Ziggurat of Ur, Iraq

Gudea Cylinders, Building of Girsu Temple, Iraq

Great Zimbabwe

ICE AGE AND UNDERWATER ANCIENT SITES

In their timeline of history, the secular world suggests that there were many ice ages, one after another in a pattern. According to biblical history however, the story is quite different. The oldest scribed book of the Bible is thought to be Job and this book makes many direct references to ice and snow (Job 6:16, 24:19, 37:6, 38:22). There are reasons to believe that some of the Old Testament saints lived during the buildup and melt down of the one great Ice Age, spanning hundreds of years. The Bible teaches that the earth is around 6,000 years old therefore the Ice Age had to fit in this time framework.

The Flood of Noah gives the mechanism to trigger the Ice Age. Most people do not understand the full impact of the Flood of Noah's day. Not only did it reshape the geography of the planet, but it would have drastically changed the climate

as well. It would be ideal conditions for an Ice Age having warm oceans and cool summers. (Many falsely think that if we cool the globe we get an ice age, but that is not accurate; we just get a cool globe, but not the ice accumulation).

The oceans would have been much warmer after the Flood due to continental movements, volcanic basalts, and other factors during and after the Flood. The result is that there would be more precipitation due to heated water causing more evaporation, particularly in winter in the forms of snow and ice. Cool summers are activated by reduced sunlight due to all the volcanism. The reason is that fine ash particles from eruptions linger in the upper atmosphere reflecting sunlight away from earth, hence a cooler earth particularly in summer months. Even modern volcanoes have caused this affect for a short term dropping global

Underwater archaeology presents a number of challenges, including money and proper training/certification of researchers as divers. But the discoveries of underwater sites like Yonaguni, Cleopatra's Palace in ancient Alexandria, Dwarka in the Bay of Cambay, Menouthis in Egypt, sites in Greece, in the North Sea, and even shipwreck evidence dating back to the fifth century B.C. preserved in the Black Sea is leading many to question the traditional timelines and understanding of ancient man.

temperatures for a time. So the mechanism is in place to have large amounts of accumulation in winter and cools summers so the ice and snow do not melt away these layers. Then the next year's accumulation builds this up further.

The rain over the equatorial regions would mean great vegetation instead of the deserts that exist today like the Gobi and Sahara. There is in fact evidence that these areas were once well watered. Riverbeds, ancient cities, and fossils of animals are found and the Bible speaks of Israel being forested with lions and bears. In the northern and southern regions, a great buildup of snow and ice created huge ice caps, some as deep as 15,000 feet. This global buildup of ice caps, taking water out of the oceans by as much as 200 feet, would cause a much lower "sea level" than today.

As the oceans cooled down after the Flood, less warm moisture-laden air moved over the continents and the great ice caps began to melt. As the climate changed, "global warming" occurred; not the popularized secular version, but a slow warming that is still taking place today following the great Flood.

WHAT DOES THIS MEAN WHEN IT COMES TO ANCIENT MAN?

The Bible says twice that God "scattered" the people of Babel. So within a short time after the Flood, tribes migrated all around the globe. The lowering of ocean levels would facilitate this and allow settlements and cities and "replicas" of Babel to be built around the equatorial regions due to the lower sea levels. As the ocean levels rose, these sites were covered and have been hidden from our view except through legends and traditions, such as Atlantis. Until recently!

New discoveries are showing Babel cultural sites deep underwater around the world. Predictions are that these discoveries will increase in number now that the knowledge that they exist are known, and this is what researchers are to look for. Artifacts and sites deep under sea level are suggested off Japan, Southern India, the Mediterranean, and in underwater caves off the coast of Costa Rica.

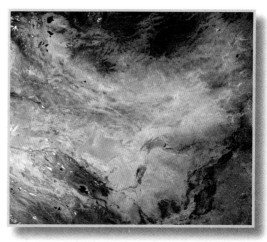

Aerial image of the Gobi desert.

Many are now suggesting Atlantis was not just a myth or even just one city, but perhaps a linked civilization spread across the world around the equator. We know there was a lot of travel around the globe long before Columbus!

KEEP ALERT AND WATCH FOR MORE DISCOVERIES!

The team at Jackson Hole Bible College desires to continue their studies of Ancient Man in the upcoming years. If you know of any subjects that might make good research, please send those comments to jhbc.admin@gmail.com. We are looking forward to hearing from you.

Now that you have considered the evidence we have presented, you might want to know what some of the driving and motivating truths are that affect our thinking.

The following list of axioms is important, sequential concepts that we have found very helpful in gaining a truly biblical perspective. More could be added to this list, yet this selection of axioms shows the truths that guide our thinking.

How you view all of life, especially the history of ancient man is determined by your view of God and His Word. These articles will show you where the researchers of JHBC were coming from and some of the distinctive basic building blocks of the one-year apologetics program at the college. Please join us as you look behind the scenes to a few of the philosophical principles behind the book...

Axioms

An axiom, as defined by Jackson Hole Bible College (JHBC), is a fact that ought to be a widely held and understood truth. This list of axioms has have defined and set apart the two-semester program at JHBC, laying a foundation for a better, more fluent understanding of the Word of God.

Axiom #1: The Bible needs to be approached as supernatural.

"But know this first of all, that no prophecy of Scripture is a matter of one's own interpretation, for no prophecy was ever made by an act of human will, but men moved by the Holy Spirit spoke from God" (2 Peter 1:20–21).

Since the Bible is an inspired text, directly from a holy and immutable God, it must be inerrant. If it were merely the ramblings of fallible men throughout the years, we would expect to find errors and contradictions, but this is not the case. From the first chapters scribed by Moses to the last prophecies written by John, the Lord divinely protects His Word by guiding the writers' hands and safeguarding the translations throughout the ages. The Bible is not an ordinary book! We can have confidence that the Word of God that we are holding today is an accurate translation of the original manuscripts because God is in control of His Scriptures.

Axiom #2: There is nothing that we know about God that He did not have to tell us.

"But a natural man does not accept the things of the Spirit of God, for they are foolishness to him; and he cannot understand them, because they are spiritually appraised" (1 Corinthians 2:14).

As sons of Adam, finite, sinful beings, we cannot understand anything about God without direct illumination from the Holy Spirit. God is infinite and therefore far beyond our understanding. ("For My thoughts are not your thoughts, nor are your ways My ways," declares the Lord, "For as the heavens are higher than the earth, so are My ways higher than your ways and My thoughts than your thoughts" Isaiah 55:8–9.) The Holy Spirit draws and quickens human beings to come to the knowledge of the Lord, but without His work, no one has the ability in himself or herself to understand anything of God.

Axiom #3: Bible prophecy confirms God.

"Declaring the end from the beginning, and from ancient times things which have not been done, saying, 'My purpose will be established, and I will accomplish all My good pleasure'" (Isaiah 46:10).

Seeing Bible prophecy fulfilled accurately, to the letter, is proof that there is a God. For God to be able to give information about the future He must be omniscient and outside of time, knowing the end from the beginning and knowing the choices that man will make. Throughout Scripture, God's prophecies, given through His prophets, are fulfilled with astonishing accuracy. Each one confirms the existence of an all-knowing God who dwells in eternity past and future.

Axiom #4: God wants to be known.	"They heard the sound of the Lord God walking in the garden in the cool of the day" (Genesis 3:8). "They shall be My people, and I will be their God" (Jeremiah 32:38). "And I heard a loud voice from the throne, saying, 'Behold the tabernacle of God is among men, and He will dwell among them, and they shall be His people, and God Himself will be among them' " (Revelation 21:3).	God desires to have fellowship with the human race that He created. The sole purpose for the creation of mankind was so that the Father would receive glory to Himself. He is a jealous God, expecting all glory to Him alone. Throughout the course of human history the Lord has actively been restoring that which was lost in the Garden of Eden. God seeks to reinstate the fellowship He had with Adam and Eve before it was destroyed by mankind's rebellion. The Bible illustrates God's desire through the chosen people Israel, the death of His only Son, and the coming kingdom in which His bride will rule with Him!
Axiom #5: When God created man, He had a challenge.	"And without faith it is impossible to please Him, for he who comes to God must believe that He is and that He is a rewarder of those who seek Him" (Hebrews 11:6). "For we walk by faith, not by sight" (2 Corinthians 5:7). "So faith comes from hearing, and hearing by the word of Christ" (Romans 10:17).	How could an infinite God reveal Himself to finite creatures in such a way that they could know Him and desire to worship Him? Saying that God had a challenge is using anthropomorphic language, meaning that God, from our human perspective, would have faced a challenge. God knew how He would reveal Himself from the beginning, and that we would not be able to know everything about Him. However, the Lord created an avenue by which a finite being may understand certain truths about God: faith. Through faith, we can rest in that which we do not understand. ("Now faith is the assurance of things hoped for, the conviction of things not seen" Hebrews 11:1.) Faith is the only way in which we are able to even remotely grasp the attributes of an eternal being.
Axiom #6: The origin of evolution is older than people realize.	"I will ascend above the heights of the clouds; I will make myself like the Most High" (Isaiah 14:14). "Your heart was lifted up because of your beauty; you corrupted your wisdom by reason of your splendor" (Ezekiel 28:17).	Though many people believe evolution started with Darwin, it actually began much earlier than that. Lucifer was created with the ability to choose and reason, chose to reject God as the one and only, and believed that he himself could become god. This was the origin of evolution; the first case of a being believing he could advance into something more sophisticated. Rooted in pride, evolution has since convinced man that he has advanced from primordial soup and is in a continual state of advancement. Satan has been deceiving men throughout the centuries that they are able to become like God, and indeed this is evident in many ancient religions and even New Age theories of today.

Axiom #7: Those who reject God as Creator are still religious.	"The fool has said in his heart, 'There is no God,' they are corrupt and have committed abominable injustice" (Psalm 53:1). "For the wrath of God is revealed from heaven against all ungodliness and unrighteousness of men who suppress the truth in unrighteousness, because that which is known about God is evident within them; for God made it evident to them" (Romans 1:18–19).	People who subscribe to Darwinian evolution often state that they believe only scientific "fact", yet they are missing an important part of their "belief". Evolution involves just as much faith, if not more, as Christianity or another religion. On the evolutionary side, the two prevailing beliefs in the origin of the universe are steady state (eternal) or big bang (that the universe created itself). If it was eternal, then why does heat still exist and stars still shine as that energy should have long been lost due to the laws of thermodynamics. But consider big bang (which there are several different big bang models), where each model has something coming from nothing. This has never been repeated nor observed! Evolutionists must believe in something that they have no evidence for and cannot support. This requires faith, thus making the evolutionist quite religious.
Axiom #8: Satan can't create, he can only pervert.	"There is a way which seems right to a man, but its end is the way of death" (Proverbs 14:12). "You are of your father the devil, and you want to do the desires of your father. He was a murderer from the beginning, and does not stand in the truth because there is no truth in him. Whenever he speaks a lie, he speaks from his own nature, for he is a liar and the father of lies" (John 8:44).	As a created and finite being, Satan is not able to create anything. The only power that Satan has is the power that the Lord has chosen to give to him. Thus, in the present times as well as in history, Satan has only been able to take that which the Lord created and pervert it in an attempt to become "like God" and deceive the nations. He has tried to distort God's message, obscure His purposes, and soil His plan. Yet because Satan must always work from something that originated from God, his deceptions can always be traced back to a truth that was created by God.
Axiom #9: Satan is the ultimate counterfeiter.	"I will ascend above the heights of the clouds; I will make myself like the Most High" (Isaiah 14:14).	Because of the previous axiom, "Satan can't create, he can only pervert," everything he does is a counterfeit of something in God's plan. Satan seeks to take the glory away from the Lord by creating his own story. He instigates his own counterfeit religions, plans, and purposes that resemble God's, yet ends up destroying the lives of those who are deceived by him. Yet his counterfeit will not prevail. At the end of the world, after the sinners have been judged and found guilty, they will all bow down at the name of Jesus (Phil. 2:10–11).

Axiom #10: There is a priority of God in all things.	"For by Him all things were created, both in the heavens and on earth, visible and invisible, whether thrones or dominions or rulers or authorities — all things have been created through Him and for Him. He is before all things, and in Him all things hold together" (Colossians 1:16–17). "I am the Alpha and the Omega, the first and the last, the beginning and the end" (Revelation 22:13).	Since God dwells in eternity past and exists outside of time, since He is the Creator and Author of all things, since He is omniscient, omnipotent and omnipresent, He has priority. Whether it's His version of history over the pagan authors' or His plan for worship over the cultic religions, He is the ultimate authority. As we have stated previously, the beginning of all information is founded in the Lord and in knowing Him personally. Throughout history, Satan has been perverting God's message and trying to thwart God's plans on earth, and many important originals have been corrupted. Yet we must not just look at the perversion — we must take a step back and look for God's original purpose for those areas that have been defiled. Remember that God had an intended design for many objects and subjects, but we only recognize them now because of their perversions. Because God is priority, His purpose supersedes all other influences, whether the world says they have authority or not.
Axiom #11: There are only two possible worldviews.	Matthew 7:13–27	In the Sermon on the Mount, Jesus gives several examples to illustrate that there are only two kingdoms/religions in this world: the kingdom of God the Father and the counterfeit kingdom of Satan. The two religions are depicted as the narrow and wide gates, the good and bad trees, and the foundation of rock or sand. These two religions — one that originates from God, one that goes against everything He is — cannot mix. A Christian can't live in both worlds! Either we will be partaking of the good tree (when we are walking in the Spirit) or we will be partaking of the bad tree when following the schemes of the world. Recognizing the different elements of Satan's kingdom will provide for us a kind of immunity, an ability to perceive counterfeit more easily. As Christians, we must become so familiar with the Word of God that we quickly recognize the counterfeit when we are confronted with it in our daily lives and not fall into the lies of the false kingdom.
Axiom #12: Christians today are living like pagans because their feet are on two different foundations.	". . . being a double-minded man, unstable in all his ways" (James 1:8).	As Christians, we must believe on Jesus Christ's atonement for our sins as Redeemer and yet we so often forget about placing our faith in Him as Creator. Many believers wholeheartedly proclaim the gospel while denouncing the first chapters of the Bible as fiction. Not only are there theological problems with this standpoint, but also it affects the way you live. No man is able to stand upon such contradictory foundations. Trying to meld two opposing worldviews is personally destructive.

Axiom #13: People's theology and practice pendulum swing because they do not understand antinomies.		As finite creatures, we must understand and take by faith the fact that we will not be able to understand all things about God. As we study, we will "bump" into some of God's infinite, sovereign, and immutable attributes that will cause contradictions in our own minds. Often there may seem to be more questions than answers. Antinomies occur when there are two truths presented in the Bible that seem to contradict each other. Things such as human responsibility and God's election, the command to pray and God's sovereignty, or Jesus' status as God-man can cause people to stumble in their faith or pursue a bad theology. By choosing one truth over the other, you are forced to reject or reinterpret Scriptures to fit your view. It is very important to understand the practical application of an antinomy. By faith you can accept both seemingly opposing ideas to be equally true and therefore grasp the message of the various texts of Scripture.
Axiom #14: God wants us to know about the future.	"Declaring the end from the beginning, and from ancient times things which have not been done, saying, 'My purpose will be established, and I will accomplish all My good pleasure' " (Isaiah 46:10).	At the time of its writing, the Bible was 43 percent prophetic. It is clear from this fact alone that God desires us to have knowledge of the future. He does not want us to stick our heads in the sand and ignore the world around us, unconcerned about what is going to happen. We are called to live in the mindset that this world is not our home (Hebrews 11:13–16). Many prophecies have not yet been fulfilled, so we can still be looking forward with some knowledge of what is to come. We are called to be a discerning people, a people who understand the times that we live in. "Of the sons of Issachar, men who understood the times, with knowledge of what Israel should do" (1Chron. 12:32).
Axiom #15: Christians today have been taught thousands of unrelated facts that make them susceptible to every wind of doctrine.	"How I did not shrink from declaring to you anything that was profitable, and teaching you publicly and from house to house" (Acts 20:20). "Be diligent to present yourself approved to God as a workman who does not need to be ashamed, accurately handling the word of truth" (2 Timothy 2:15).	As a Christian in this world full of deceptions and counterfeits, we must constantly discern between truth and error, so that we are remaining true to the Word of God. Yet through many Sunday school lessons and church services, the average Christian is taught fact upon fact of Scripture in such a way that the facts seem disconnected and not applicable to daily life. Christians need to learn their Bibles, learn how God wrote the different genres and learn the nuances of the different languages. We need to learn the time-line of the Bible, the overall "big picture," so that when presented with new information, we know where to place it. God's Word can never be exhausted, each verse has connections all over the rest of Scripture, and yet if we do not understand these interlocking ideas, it makes doctrine hard to understand. Knowing where the facts fit helps you to defend your beliefs and seek out the truth.

Axiom #16:
The Hebrews had a different learning system than the Greeks.

The Hebrew learning system teaches the "universals" first and works down to the particulars. In contrast, the Greek practice is to focus on the particulars and then build upon the foundation until finally you reach the universals. The Bible is written largely for the Hebrew mind. It starts with God, the universal, and works down to the particulars of daily living. Looking at the overall scheme of the Bible, the universals are taught starting in Genesis, and then toward the end of the New Testament, the Apostle Paul describes the particulars of daily living. Thus, if we do not understand the universal foundation that is laid out in Genesis 1–11, how can we properly store the information that we are taught later in the Bible? Genesis 1–11 is literally the foundation of the Bible.

Axiom #17:
Learning must be repetitive.

"For He says, 'Order on order, order on order, line on line, line on line, a little here, a little there'" (Isaiah 28:10).

For certain teachings to stick and make an impact in our lives, we must be taught the principle again and again from Scripture. We are in a continual state of learning, even focusing on the same thing time and time again, so that the lesson will be driven deep into our soul. God made us with this need for repetitive instruction, and therefore educates us through repetitive methods in His Word and in life. Hopefully sooner, rather than later, we will learn our lesson.

Axiom #18:
All goes back to the nature and character of God.

The authority structure for our lives follows several simple steps:

▷ Precept: The statement of right or wrong — the rule given in precept form

▷ Principle: The reason behind the precept

▷ Person: The Person of God who stands behind the principle

In our instruction we must not shy away from teaching the whole counsel of God. We must teach the specific commands and instructions of the Lord as well as the reason why we should follow these commands and live a certain way. Unfortunately, many times we only teach the precept or the principle and forget to point everything back to the character and nature of God, the ultimate motivator and instigator of all principles and precepts.

Axiom #19: An immutable God demands absolutes.		Relating to the previous axiom, yet expounding upon it, the character and nature of God, being unchanging and immutable, requires that His people live their lives according to absolutes. If the God that we served was a changing, ever-fluctuating God, we would have no reason to hold to absolutes, yet we must realize that our God is the same yesterday, today, and forever (Hebrews 13:8). There are no gray areas with a God of perfect justice and righteousness. Our God is good and without error, and therefore He defines right and wrong. There can be no arguments.
Axiom #20: The Bible is sufficient.	"All Scripture is inspired by God and profitable for teaching, for reproof, for correction, for training in righteousness; so that the man of God may be adequate, equipped for every good work" (2 Timothy 3:16–17).	Through the imparting of the Scriptures, God has given to mankind all that he needs to live his life to the praise and glory of God. "Seeing that His divine power has granted to us everything pertaining to life and godliness, through the true knowledge of Him who called us by His own glory and excellence" (2 Peter 1:3). We do not need further revelation for our lives to be successful. The Lord has promised that if we are faithful in studying and applying that which He has given us, we will be prepared for whatever trials we experience in this life.
Axiom #21: The best hermeneutic for studying Scripture . . .		To correctly understand and apply Scripture, we need a consistent pair of glasses through which we interpret God's Word. A literal, historical, grammatical, and contextual approach to the Word of God is the only hermeneutic that will provide a reliable interpretation of the text. We must take the time and read the passage in context; we must understand what was being said according to the original languages; and we must consider the historical context around the time that the book was written. We generally take the literal reading of the text instead of a figurative meaning. So many times believers will use the cut, copy, and paste method for determining truth. We do not enjoy being convicted by Scripture and so we take the liberty of discarding that which we deem unnecessary. By doing so, we are placing ourselves over God, and interpreting His truth according to our own authority. This is unacceptable! Examine your hermeneutic and be sure that you are interpreting Scripture as it should be and not to fit your own desires.

DEATH AND DECAY

The Bible teaches that the original creation was perfect and then Adam sinned, bringing decay, chaos, thorns, pain, and death into the world. It also teaches that in the future there will be no death (Isaiah 25:8).

In contrast, the secular worldview goes something like this: "According to the fossil record, life evolved over millions of years" — nothing supernatural, nothing "perfect." And you Christians everywhere are accepting this "fact" of science. You are saying God used millions of years to create everything and then He said it was very good (Genesis 1:31). Yet according to this view, when Adam ate the fruit, it didn't cause death because death existed previously (throughout the millions of years of evolving life forms). What then is our future hope?

So you have the supernatural creation of a perfect world versus a slow struggle through natural processes by which everything evolved. Clearly these views are contrary to each other and when you carry them out to their final conclusions, they do not coincide. Yet people try to mix them! Something is very wrong here — only one can be true.

When you try to mesh the two views, you end up with an inconsistent and faulty hermeneutic. Think about it. You have past and present death; I wonder what heaven is going to be like? Well God says there is no death and no tears (Revelation 21:4). Yet if you are going to allegorize and figuratively handle the Old Testament account of creation, to make it millions of years instead of what the text says and hermeneutically demands, then why wouldn't you use the same process of hermeneutics to define heaven? To be consistent, you must handle these texts figuratively as well. So how can you prove that there will be no *physical* tears? Because of your figurative interpretation of Genesis, you have no reason to believe that; your inconsistency gives you no hermeneutical argument to affirm that will be the case. You are picking and choosing throughout the Bible what you want to believe and how you want to interpret the texts. This is a terrible hermeneutic.

Furthermore, trying to synchronize both views results in theological issues. The Bible states: "Just as through one man sin entered into the world, and death through sin, and so death spread to all men, because all sinned" (Romans 5:12). The verse clearly states that death came to all men because of Adam. So was this physical death? Putting "millions of years" into the Bible means the consequences of Adam's sin must not include normal death. It can't, because the Bible teaches that Christ's Cross remedies Adam's sin, destroying the power of death (Hebrews 2:14). But if physical death was not a consequence of Adam's sin, then Christ's finished work cannot remedy physical death. Moreover, this would make God inconsistent. Consider this carefully: if death existed before Adam's sin, meaning that the death in the universe, as evidenced by the fossil record, was the direct result of the creative work of God, it would be totally unreasonable that the Father would make Christ die to remedy what He did. Christ's death would be inconsistent. Why would He physically die on the Cross to remedy physical death if physical death was His own work? That is almost blasphemy.

Thus the point is: If physical death existed before Adam and Eve sinned, then the physical death of Christ on the Cross has nothing to do with remedying physical death. Why would He try to fix something He did? If it was wrong, then God should own up to it. But if there was nothing wrong with it (and there couldn't be anything wrong with it because God is immutable and Holy), then by the laws of logic, Christ did nothing to fix physical death, because it wasn't wrong! Under this view, the Cross only remedied *spiritual* consequences of Adam's sin. Indeed the results of Adam's sin must have been only spiritual if the *physical* issues were already present.

So then a new problem arises: why did Jesus have to die *physically* and why would He have to resurrect *physically*? And what hope do *you* have of *physical* resurrection if the physical death that is in the universe had absolutely nothing to do with Adam's sin? Now you are not only attacking Christ, you are attacking the blood-atoning work of Christ on the cross and ultimately the character and nature of God. You are redefining everything!

As a matter of fact, look at this verse: "For since by a man came death, by a man also came the resurrection of the dead" (1 Corinthians 15:21). The first man is a reference to Adam and the second is to Christ. If Adam only brought spiritual death, then all Jesus brought is *spiritual* resurrection. If you're consistent between the two, if your hermeneutic is the same, then both must be *spiritual.* Not physical. Does anybody know what you do to New Testament orthodox doctrine when you erase the *physical, literal Resurrection of Christ*? What happens? Paul says our whole faith is in vain (1 Corinthians 15:14). Here's another verse: "For as in Adam all die, so also in Christ all will be made

alive" (1 Corinthians 15:22). If you don't believe the *physical death*, then Christ cannot give you *physical life*! And He cannot give us life unless He was first raised, and He cannot be raised unless He was first dead. So did He, or did He not, resurrect *physically*? Yes or no? Then there had to be *physical* death.

Also, the teaching of millions of years, trying to include physical death in the original creation, ruins the hope of *our* resurrection. Romans 6:23 says, "For the wages of sin is death, but the free gift of God is eternal life." So if it was only spiritual death, then don't count on having a physical resurrected body with which to enjoy the pleasures of heaven! You can just float around on a cloud!

Furthermore, the Bible tells us that death, decay, and chaos are not a natural part of creation. Consider Romans 8:19–20: "For the anxious longing of the creation waits eagerly for the revealing of the sons of God. For the creation was subjected to futility [there's the curse; there's death and decay; there's disease, chaos, pain, and suffering], not willingly, but because of Him who subjected it, in hope." So the creation was subjected to the curse; it wasn't designed to decay; it wasn't a natural part of the original creation; death wasn't inherent in it. In fact, it is Christ who subjects the world to the entropy, to the Curse. In Genesis 3, the Curse is placed, but for what purpose? *"In hope."* What does that mean? What hope? Well, God told Adam that he was going to have pain and suffering, thorns and thistles. Eve was told that she would have more pain in childbirth (Genesis 3:16–19). Why? To show them *physically,* in the *physical* world, that there are consequences to sin. Because of the Curse, we experience these consequences physically in order that we might realize that there are also spiritual consequences, *spiritual* death. Even today God uses the Curse to remind you and me that we ran from Him and we need to get back to Him. Pain, suffering, death, and decay are a testimony, a witness of our sin that should convince us of how much we need forgiveness. The trials of this life should have us running to the grace and *life* that He offers. God has used the Curse as a blessing! What an incredible thought! However, if the secular view is right, if all the physical death was already here, then how could God use it to remind Adam and Eve, and all successive generations, that it was a result of their sin?

But you say, "It isn't that big of a deal, I can still find Jesus as my Savior." Yes, that may be, but what about the next generation? When you redefine Jesus using this system, He becomes whatever the secular world says He is. Once this happens, the gospel becomes irrelevant. Without Jesus, the one, true Jesus there is no saving power in the gospel. In John 14:6 Jesus makes this clear: "I am the way, the truth, and the life; no one comes to the Father but through Me." And it is only through His death and Resurrection that this is possible.

The writer of Hebrews sums this whole issue up: "Therefore, since the children share in the flesh and blood, He Himself likewise also partook of the same, that through death He might render powerless him who had the power of death, that is, the devil. . . . Therefore, He had to be made like His brethren in all things, so that He might become a merciful and faithful high priest in things pertaining to God, to make propitiation for the sins

of the people" (Hebrews 2:14–17). There was a *physical* death because Christ had a *physical* body. Therefore, there had to be a physical resurrection. And through Christ's death and resurrection, He made propitiation for our sins, so death had to come from Adam and Eve's sin originally or it makes no sense theologically. Finally, if death came from Adam's sin, then there could be no "millions of years" of death and decay *before* Adam! Logic demands this process of cause and effect.

So "millions of years" is an attack on Scripture, the person and attributes of God, and the attributes of Christ, His work on the cross, and His resurrection. It is also an attack on our future, because Christ holds up the resurrection as the ultimate goal and hope for us. He tells us that someday we are going to be resurrected, too, *physically*. So which Adam is non-essential to the gospel message? You must have the original Adam, the original prefect creation and the fall of man introducing death and decay. You must have a consistent hermeneutic approach to interpreting the entire Bible, for you have seen what happens when you re-translate even one key verse of the Bible — dominoes fall everywhere you turn, everything gets diluted and distorted. Again and again, God takes things back to Genesis, founding principles on the truths that were revealed there. It's time we should, too!

Interested in further study?

We bring you these final words of caution. There are many internet sites to go to, as well as resource books, tapes, videos, and museums that have interesting presentations of data about ancient man. There is an almost constant flow of TV specials from Discovery, History II, Nova, and more, with many programs using the keyword "mysteries." With the tremendous search for spirituality, this curiosity in ancient things can be evidenced through the growing interest in the mystical past.

Some people believe that they can find answers in history that will guide them in the future. There seems to be a fixation on ancient times, and we have noticed a behind-the-scenes motive in the study and pursuit of these "mysteries." We have been convinced there is an agenda. Many gurus believe mankind and the world have gone through cycles. They hold that we are entering a new age. In their view ancient men secreted away information for us to discover so we can insure our survival as we enter this time of change marked by chaos and great cataclysmic events. This new age agenda (which is really not new) is woven in many of the secular literatures on the subject.

We propose this is a counterfeit in itself and smoke screen to hide the true coming of judgment on our world and our accountability to the God who created all things. We believe their presuppositions are wrong, their starting points incorrect, and thus their conclusions are misguided at best.

But the actual real data they are unearthing and cataloging can be valuable. These new discoveries of early man do not destroy our faith; they can actually affirm it. Many discoveries of real cities, empires, mounds, etc., are being made all the time. Christians have no purpose in avoiding these or playing the ostrich by sticking our heads in the sand. We should not fear the unearthing of sound evidences in regard to ancient civilizations, for these amazing discoveries often fit perfectly in the schematic of the history of man and the earth in the biblical record.

We also have noticed that there are some non-believers who honestly take seriously and accept the reality of the intelligence of early man as we do. Unlike so many evolutionists who simply ignore the data, these people do not deny or avoid it. They do not give up on evolution, however, as the origin of man but simply push it back thousands of years earlier than most evolutionists speculate it took place. Some even hold that mankind was "seeded" here from other civilizations. They too still hold to evolution; one that simply began on a different planet.

So we need to be cautious of agendas, motives, false and incorrect assumptions and staring points. We need to guard our hearts carefully and be strengthened through Paul's edifying message to the church at Corinth: "We are destroying speculations and every lofty thing raised up against the knowledge of God, and we are taking every thought captive to the obedience of Christ" (2 Corinthians 10:5).

We hope our work has given you an understanding of a biblical view which will help you discern fact from fiction and will give you a spiritual immunity to the purposes and motives behind so much of the ancient man agenda. May you be encouraged to familiarize yourself with the concepts we have put forward and use them in your apologetic ministry of giving an answer for your faith.

"...sanctify Christ as Lord in your hearts, always being ready to make a defense to everyone who asks you to give an account for the hope that is in you, yet with gentleness and reverence" (1 Peter 3:15).

—*The Ancient Man Research Team*

 *Pastor Don Landis* is the president of Jackson Hole Bible College and serves as pastor/teacher of Community Bible Church. He is also the founding chairman of the board of Answers in Genesis and a graduate of Moody Bible Institute. He has been teaching on ancient man subjects for many years at JHBC. He and his wife Beverly live in Jackson Hole, Wyoming where they live with their two daughters, son-in-laws and families.

 *Analea Styles* has a passion for writing and reaching people with the truth, using the gifts God has blessed her with to bring Him glory through the written word. Analea grew up in British Columbia, Canada and attended Jackson Hole Bible College for their one year Biblical Foundations program, graduating in 2011. She joined the Ancient Man Research Project as primary wordsmith, working with the team throughout the writing and editing process.

 *Derrick Zuk* is the communications specialist for Jackson Hole Bible College, working primarily with audio visual/internet technologies. His passion is to disciple others and use these skills for God's glory in the ministry. Derrick grew up in upstate New York, moving to Russia with his family in 2003 when his parents became missionaries. In 2010, he attended Jackson Hole Bible College where he earned his Biblical Foundations diploma.

 *Josh Gilmore* is the administrative assistant to pastor Don Landis, and he also serves as operations coordinator for the Bible College where he enjoys working with the administration of JHBC. Josh grew up in Kansas and graduated from JHBC in the spring of 2007. He has a desire to personally disciple students to a stronger and more faithful walk with the Lord. Josh was the primary coordinator between the researchers, publisher, and design teams.

 *Brian Mariani* is a researcher for the Ancient Man project, with a bachelor of science teaching degree, and a degree of biblical foundations from JHBC. He resides with his wife Aimee, and works in the Midwest as a high school science teacher.

 *Bethany Youngblood* also served as part of the project's research team. Ancient civilizations have captivated this Florida native since she was small. Her desire is to write historical fiction and give God the glory through her life and work.

 *John Burnside* lives with his wife, Hannah, and son in Jackson, Wyoming. He graduated from JHBC in 2005. He works as youth leader at Community Bible Church, administrator for Jackson Hole Christian Academy and is a Certified Apple Computer Technician. He has enjoyed studying the sciences for almost 20 years. John loves to see God's handiwork in creation.

CONNECTING CHRISTIANS
who believe in Biblical Creation.

forums | blogs | groups | resources | and more!

CreationConversations.com

"In invaluable tool for the defense of the Christian faith."

Dr. John Mccarther, Jr.

The
HENRY MORRIS
STUDY BIBLE

APOLOGETICS COMMENTARY
and EXPLANATORY NOTES *from the*
'FATHER *of* MODERN CREATIONISM'

King James Version

Black Genuine Leather - **$94.99** | 978-0-89051-658-4

Casebound - **$39.99** | 978-0-89051-657-7

Over **10,000** study notes from Dr. Morris on over **2200** pages of text with a **10 pt** font.
Concordance – **22** Appendices – Full-Color Maps

The Henry Morris Study Bible is truly one of a kind. No other resource offers the comprehensive analysis of biblical creation and authority of Scripture that this one presents.

Master
Books®
A Division of New Leaf Publishing Group

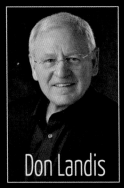
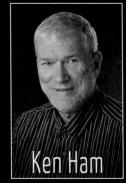